Yes to Career Success! For Women in Transition

by

Candace A. Hennekens

PS & P

ProWriting Services and Press

 Published by ProWriting Services and Press, 415 Terrill Street, Chippewa Falls, Wisconsin 54729.
Telephone: 715/723-8799.

Printed in the United States of America.
First printing, soft cover.

ISBN 0-9630148-1-1

Library of Congress Catalog Card Number 92-96836

This book is dedicated to Ron, Anne, and Jennifer,
for their love and support.

Table of Contents

Introduction

The old rules about work don't apply anymore. Headlines proclaim another layoff. Secure jobs are non-existent. Unemployment statistics receive front page news coverage. Re-entry or entry into the work place has never been as difficult. Yet the work place today continues to provide many opportunities for satisfying work. The difference is that you have to adapt to the new rules.

You will have to be willing to capitalize on new trends resulting from demographic changes, technological advances, the transformation of our economy from manufacturing to a service and information-oriented economy, new roles for women, and the growing importance of small business in fostering prosperity. You will have to take responsibility for shaping a working career that will require you to grow, learn, and change as the world around you changes. You will have to believe that it is possible to be successful and you will have to take charge in order to find something satisfying in the work place. By using the changing forces, and becoming a planner, you can find a satisfying niche for your unique skills and knowledge in today's work place. A fresh approach will help you chart a course.

This book is intended to be a guidebook, offering up a menu of potential choices, choices you may not have previously considered because some are "non-traditional" roles for women, or options that have not been discussed in traditional career planning manuals and classes. The best approach to this book is to read it through, select the options you find appealing, and investigate your choices. The rewards are there for you, but you will have to work harder than ever before to find them. The payoff is that you will make a satisfying life for yourself.

This book is aimed at women who are in a state of transition, voluntarily or involuntarily. You may be one of the displaced homemakers who are divorced or widowed and need to seek employment for the first time. You may be a woman who has not up to this point in time taken her employment history seriously but are now understanding the long term commitment you have to work. You may be looking for increased financial reward. You may feel a lack of challenge or satisfaction with your current job. Technical obsolescence in your present career field may be around the corner. High unemployment in your career field or your geographical area may be forcing you to assess your status. You may want to turn a hobby into a career. You may have left your former employer because of a normal, early, or forced retirement but still want to continue working. You may be a recent college graduate with only a vague idea of what to do next. Or you may simply want to change your life and develop an intentional plan that puts you in charge of your life.

More and more women are part of the labor force. Since 1900, the percent of the female population age 16 and over employed has tripled, from 18.8% in 1900 to 57.5% in 1989. By the year 2000, the Census Bureau estimates that 62.6% of females age 16 and over will be employed. More and more women are figuring out that they will work until retirement, possibly beyond retirement age. The American Dream for married women also requires working. Since 1960, the percentage of married females working has jumped from 31.9% to 57.8% in 1989.

No matter what your personal circumstances or why you find yourself there, the opportunities are there for you. The road map to success means gaining a better understanding of what you want, what the opportunities are, how you can prepare for them, get the job you want, and maintain your employment status. Your self-awareness and your understanding of your options will give you the direction you need to get going on a personal plan that will enhance and improve your life. You will place working in perspective and learn its value to you. In the process you will become a planner and develop an attitude of continually assessing your options and where you want to be. Your life will become more in balance so that all elements of your life—work, spiritual, and personal—provide you with satisfaction, and you will learn how to maintain that balance as life circumstances change and you find you need to adapt again. For change we must. Today's world offers an array of options and fast turns and evolving paths. A satisfying life can be created when you understand that there is no such thing as one way, one sure way, or one path that will last forever.

Chapter One

Become Career-Minded

As long as you must work, expand your thinking beyond having a job into having a job that is a career. A career is the high road to independence and control. It gives you choices as well as opportunities to develop your talents and abilities to make an exciting, satisfying life rather than being a prisoner in a job that is not satisfying.

Job and Career Defined

If you look up the word job in the dictionary, you'll see it comes from Middle English, originally meaning mouthful. The dictionary defines job as a piece of work, anything one has to do, or a position of employment. A job supports you, pays the bills, puts food on the table, but is something you're eager to leave at the end of the working day. On the other hand, the word career derives from the Latin word meaning wagon road or path. The dictionary gives several definitions, including one's progress through life; one's advancement or achievement in a particular vocation; a lifework; profession; occupation. People such as doctors, lawyers, writers, teachers, and news broadcasters are described as having careers.

There is a difference between career and job. Individual jobs over a period of time can add up to a career if there is linkage between skills and knowledge used. But often jobs are just positions of employment. You could waitress at an endless number of restaurants and still be a waitress. You could type an endless number of letters and still be a clerk/typist. The difference between career and a job is also accentuated by the feeling of satisfaction you derive from the work. In addition, there are usually differences in pay because jobs are at the low end of the totem pole. There is also a difference in stature and status. A career gives you pride, reflecting your progress in life.

The number of careers is endless. One can have a career in law enforcement, in office administration, as an accountant, in the food services business, or in engineering, to name a few.

Some careers are based on distinct bodies of knowledge that must be acquired in order to practice: such as medicine, law, real estate. Those careers are more accurately called professions and often require passing examinations that measure whether you have the required knowledge and/or adherence to a code of ethics.

A career is the building up of skills and knowledge from position to position, overlapping to create expertise and broad and specific knowledge in a paid position. For example, a job as a typist leading to a position as an administrative secretary leading to a position as an office administrator is a career.

Elements in a Career

Several elements must be present to have a career. The first element is a steady progression from one position to another which builds on the knowledge and skills used in that position for knowledge and skills needed in the next. There is a pattern to the positions and they complete a person's understanding of a particular area so that you have a broad understanding of a certain field. The symbol of an upside down pyramid conceptualizes this concept. Each step up builds on previous layers so that, at the top, you understand most aspects of a selected field. If, when you graduated from college, you took a job as a public relations assistant, you would have mastered the techniques of writing press releases and developing mailing lists. When you got promoted to media representative, you learned how to communicate with the media and answer their questions. You may have then advanced to working on annual and quarterly financial reports for the company. By the time you became a manager, you had done most of the discrete tasks in the work unit so you had an in-depth as well as broad understanding of the work of the department.

A commonly made mistake is to jump from one job to another without looking for linkages of skills and knowledge between positions of employment. Employers look for linkages between job requirements and candidate skills and knowledge when they hire. They are more willing to hire a candidate for a fulltime secretarial position in the benefits department who had a previous position doing correspondence and routine typing as well as benefits work. That new secretarial position specializing in benefits might then lead to an entry level benefits administration position, which could lead up a career path.

The second element for a career is a natural interest and talent and desire to do the work required of the position. When you want to do something rather than have to do something, you are able to take the bad with the good. You bring energy to the work that drives you to do your best, to keep going when you feel discouraged or overwhelmed by the challenge. You work for the challenge and excitement that the position can give. While no position is always exciting and rewarding, and work is called work because it takes your energy, the general feeling of a career-oriented woman is satisfaction and interest in the work. You feel like you are contributing and you enjoy doing it. If you do not feel this way, something about the work goes against your natural tendencies and interests and creates tension for you.

You will never be as successful doing something you don't enjoy as you will doing something you enjoy. You must have your heart in your work to do your best.

Career Planning Issues for Women

Career planning is difficult for both men and women. But for women, career planning is complicated by children. Women must plan for and manage the interruptions children bring. Many women find they are single parents with wage-earning and child-raising responsibilities conflicting. Married women also face the conflict. Women have only recently viewed career planning as a key question in their lives. Men have always identified very closely with their work. For women, the question of what to do with their lives has often been answered by the people in their lives rather than themselves. Husbands and children place demands. Many women never question that they should be asking "What is it I want?" when making decisions based on the events of their lives.

The truth of the matter is that you probably plan better menus and social activities than you plan your career. This reactionary stance on career planning prevents you from finding out what you really want to do with your life, and robs you of fulfillment, achieving your potential, satisfaction, and higher levels of income. You need to be proactive and be in charge of your life, carefully considering your options and making decisions. You must be in charge of your life in order to get out of life what you want. By considering personal, family, spiritual and working goals, you can develop a balanced, satisfying life.

Children can present obstacles when it comes to employment. They're a responsibility and need care and attention. By carefully researching child care options, and finding a reputable child care provider, a woman can provide high quality care. Ask your friends about their arrangements and find alternatives for sick child care before you start your job search. Referral agencies to help you locate child care might exist in your community. More services are available today than ever before for children in school with before and after school care options. Some employers are even enlightened enough to provide on-site child care, child care subsidies, and sick child care facilities. Research what is available to you. Learning about your options will give you choices.

Ideal Career Planning

Ideally career planning does not look at work as a separate activity into which all the energy and drive is poured and personal and family aspects of life are sacrificed. Career/life planning can accommodate other needs and strives for balance in all the areas that make life fulfilling: home, community, religious activity, personal interests as well as work.

Career/life planning takes a long term view of life and recognizes that there are life stages. Each stage may meet one need but not another. However, over the long run, you as a whole have achieved your goals. Career/life planning helps interruptions become pauses along one of the paths. Remember there is no one right way except the way you create and choose for yourself.

Career/life planning presupposes that the purpose of career/life planning is not to reach high, but to broaden and deepen knowledge and skills and personal contributions to achieve life satisfaction. With the baby boom generation competing for positions, with companies shrinking their workforces, opportunities to move up in the organization are decreasing. Therefore taking a broader view insures your satisfaction, the true measure of success, when the external measures of success may be limited.

Your Attitude Towards Work

One of the prerequisites for being successful in the work place is our own attitude towards that activity. Today there is an attitude that work is something inherently unpleasant and something we do in order to enjoy our leisure time. Not too long ago, the boundary between work and play was blurry and people enjoyed their work because work was their life. Today workers are alienated from the companies that employ them because although we work for a living, the fruits of our labor are indirect. The fruits provide us with money which we use to pay our rent, buy our groceries, purchase clothing, and other necessities. In days gone by, many people worked directly for some or all of the necessities, by farming, raising cattle, sewing their own clothes, taking care of the horse that would pull the wagon into town. Because of that, they saw a direct correlation between work and the enjoyment of life.

Regarding work as something inherently unpleasant is in and of itself an attitude that is a guarantee for unhappiness in that activity. Work provides all of us with a feeling of contributing to society, a sense of well being, a social framework for our lives, and gives us new and challenging experiences. If you regard work as inherently unpleasant and accept the premise that work will always be that way, you are robbing yourself of one of the joys of living. You will accept a job that is not suited to you. You will be more likely to stay on a job that you do not like because the job is meeting your low expectation of what it will provide you.

If, on the other hand, you believe that work can be pleasant, fulfilling, and enjoyable, you are ready to find the job and career that will provide you with much satisfaction. You will be less willing to stay on a job that you do not like, and less willing to accept a position that you think you will not like. Our expectations about an activity set the tone for the activity.

What Makes for Enjoyment

Recent studies on what makes life enjoyable have isolated the characteristics of "flow" experiences. Flow experiences are experiences so enjoyable and rewarding that people are willing to expend energy simply to be able to feel them. Flow consists of eight major components coming together in an activity. The first characteristic is that the activity is something we have a chance of completing. We must also be able to concentrate on what we are doing. The concentration is usually possible because the task undertaken has clear goals and provides immediate feedback. When engaged in flow, you are acting with a deep but effortless involvement that removes the worries and frustrations of everyday life from your consciousness, i.e. you lose yourself in the activity. Enjoyable experiences allow people to exercise a sense of control over their actions and concern for the self disappears, yet paradoxically the sense of self emerges stronger after the flow experience is over. Finally, the sense of time duration is altered: hours pass by in minutes, and minutes can stretch out to seem like hours. The combination of all these elements causes a sense of deep enjoyment that is so rewarding people feel that expending a great deal of energy is worthwhile simply to be able to feel it.[1] Studies also show that despite the fact that work provides more flow experiences than leisure activity, people still want to hurry home and have leisure time, often spent in passive activities like TV watching which provides none of the elements of the flow experience.

While some jobs provide more of the flow experience than others, what researchers found was that some individuals could create flow by the way they approached their job, even creating challenges where others saw none. The opposite was also true. Some individuals could engage in a job that had all the elements to foster flow and yet be driven crazy by their job. It is clear then that our personal motivation and our personally set goals can help us determine what is satisfying and meaningful.

Why bother you ask? Because you will spend a large portion of your life working. In fact the number of hours Americans spend working as opposed to engaged in leisure activities is going up, not down. In 1989, American workers put in hours equalling an extra month of work for that year compared to 1969. Work is a fact of life. The chances of you winning the lottery and retiring a millionaire are next to none. Anyway many lottery winners choose to continue to work because they enjoy what they are doing. Approaching your work with the right attitude will enhance your overall life and make it worth living.

In the book W*orking: People Talk About What They Do All Day and How They Feel About What They Do,* Studs Terkel talked to American workers about how they feel about their jobs. His book is about "...a search, too, for daily meaning as well as daily bread, for recognition, as well as cash, for astonishment rather than torpor, in short, for a sort of life rather than a Monday through Friday sort of dying." [2]

Dolores Dante, a waitress for 23 years in the same restaurant, was not typical in her remarks about her work. She liked being a waitress. She had set goals, saw challenge and opportunity to be the best waitress and took pride in her efforts. She obtained flow from being a waitress because of her attitude towards her work. She said:

> Some don't care. When the plate is down, you can hear the sound. I try not to have that sound. I want my hands to be right when I serve. I pick up a glass, I want it to be just right. I get to be almost Oriental in the serving. I like it to look nice, all the day. To be a waitress, it's an art. I feel like a ballerina, too. I have to go between those tables, between those chairs...Maybe that's the reason I always stayed slim. It is a certain way I can go through a chair no one else can do. I do it with an air. If

I drop a fork, there is a certain way I pick it up. I know they can tell how delicately I do it. I'm on stage.

Freud said that love and work (lieben und arbeiten) are the two moving impulses of humankind. Surely you will benefit by examining your feelings about work and creating the right soil to grow the activity that will consume so much of your energy and time. Taking charge of your work life can make it more likely that working will be a happy and strong activity for you. Work can be appropriate to your needs. Work can add to your overall quality of life. You can approach work as adding value to your life and still pursue an active, interesting, balanced total life. It need not be either an all consuming activity or a totally boring proposition. It can give you joy, satisfaction, and pleasure just as leisure time activities, family relationships, and spiritual activities nurture you.

It's Never Too Late

It is never too late to get a fresh start! Here are some stories of women who did just that.

Kate Waller Barrett, a leader in opening homes for unwed mothers, was nearly thirty and the mother of seven children in 1886 when she decided to go to medical school. Because of work with prostitutes in helping her minister husband, when she got her medical degree, she helped them find a place to have a dignified pregnancy.

Ruth Benedict, who wrote pioneering studies in cultural psychology including the book *Pattern of Culture* didn't begin her career until she was thirty-four years old.

Phyllis Diller was a homemaker. She made her professional comic debut at the age of thirty-seven.

Isak Dinesen (whom the movie "Out Of Africa" was about) published her first book at the age of forty-nine. It was called *Seven Gothic Tales*.

Katherine Gibbs, founder of the first school for secretaries bearing her name, was a widow with two sons when at forty-three she founded the school in Providence, Rhode Island.

Grandma Moses (Anna Mary Robertson Moses) took up oil painting at the age of seventy-eight when her fingers became too stiff to embroider. She won fame for her primitive or "naive" paintings. In 1960 at the age of 100, she illustrated an edition of *'Twas the Night Before Christmas.*[3]

These women are famous now, but there are millions of American woman who have gone back to work and at some point decided that they needed to take charge of their lives. All of them, famous or not, share a common characteristic: they decided that work had something to offer them, and they to offer it, and they gained a sense of happiness, satisfaction, and well being that made it worth the effort to find something enjoyable.

Behaviors That Will Make You Successful on the Job

Careful thought and planning can go a long way to making you successful. In addition, there are some behaviors on the job that will improve your success on the job as well. First of all, have a strong work ethic. All bosses like the employees who put in a full day's work for a day's pay. These employees are punctual, respect breaks and meal time starts and stops, and work, work, work. Plan your use of time so that is wisely spent. If you work hard, you'll be productive and all bosses know who their most productive employees are.

If you remember, too, that by making your boss look good, you'll look good, you'll also succeed. Make your boss's job as easy as you can. If you don't understand what you are supposed to do, ask questions. If you have a suggestion, make it. Then let your boss decide if it should be implemented. Express yourself clearly and courteously, and you'll find that you will get approached by your boss for your opinions and suggestions. Strive to take a problem-solving approach to problems. The employee who helps solve problems demonstrates a winning attitude.

Be flexible about change. Someone who is willing to try something and give it a fair trial, or come up with a better way of working will be a preferred employee over someone who is always ready to fight every change and put up roadblocks. Being adaptable will help you progress. The adaptable employees will be offered new opportunities. If you take them, you will profit.

Think for yourself. Don't listen to the factory or office scuttlebutt or disgruntlement. In the long run, you will come out ahead by forming your own opinions and will receive recognition for your leadership abilities.

At the same time, make friends and network. Talk to the people that always know what is really going on. They can provide you with helpful insights and information. Observe how other employees handle problems and situations and learn from those who are most successful at their jobs. You will learn how to solve problems in your company's environment.

Always keep learning. Learn formally through classes, either credit or non-credit. Take time to read in your field and keep up with current events as well. Be curious and feed your curiosity. Lifelong learning is necessary to advance in today's world with so much knowledge being added daily. If you keep learning, you'll never get outdated or rusty. You'll find you're more creative, better at problem-solving, and advancing on the job.

Finally, do the best job you can. The best way to get a promotion is to do the best job you can with the job you have now. The saying that you have to know the right people simply isn't true. If you truly are good at your work, you'll get noticed.

By having a plan and being flexible about your career when change occurs, you will find that you are finding satisfaction and fulfillment in your work. You'll bring home a bigger paycheck, feel pride in your accomplishments, and you will be able to live independently on your own resources if you have to or want to.

This gives you freedom through choices. This makes you feel good about yourself.

RECOMMENDATIONS FOR FURTHER WORK

1. Spend time thinking about your current job. Do you like it? What parts don't you like?
2. If you think you need some help getting the answers, make an appointment with some type of career counselor to begin the process. You can find counselors listed in the Yellow Pages under "Career and Vocational Counseling."
3. Visit your public library and read magazine articles and books on the subject of career planning and job markets. If you cannot find what you want, ask the librarian to help you.

[1] Csikszentmihalyi, Mihaly. *Flow: The Psychology of Optimal Experience.* New York: HarperPerennial, 1991, p. 49.
[2] Terkel, Studs. *Working: People Talk About What They Do All Day and How They Feel About What They Do.* New York: Pantheon, 1972, p. xi.
[3] Weiser, Marjorie P.K. and Jean S. Arbeiter. *Womanlist.* New York: Atheneum, 1981, pp. 113-114.

Chapter Two

Developing a Career Plan

Goals are a powerful tool for taking charge of your life. The dreams you dream, the wishes you wish can become your reality through goals. Goals are powerful because goals channel your energy into the direction you have set. If you do not set direction, your energy will be dispersed in many different ways. By channeling your energy, you will get what you want.

Values as the Foundation of Goals

To truly achieve your dreams, wishes, and desires, you need to go through the process of figuring out your values. Values are the most important beliefs you hold. You are being asked to make conscious decisions about how you want to live rather than react to the circumstances of your life and be passive about choices. You may have deferred to others on choices for so long that this may not be easy. You may have let others and circumstances in your life decide many of these important issues. You may feel so weighted down by your obligations and responsibilities that you think there is no room in your life for what you truly dream about and desire. "How can I pursue my dreams?", you ask, as you tend to your children, cook and clean, and go to work everyday to pay a steady stream of bills.

Not to pursue your dreams and desires is a great disservice to yourself. You are denying your creative, human part. You will not feel good about yourself if you are not directing your life towards your creative impulses which flow from your dreams and desires. To pursue your dreams and desires feels good. It makes life tolerable where it might be intolerable when you feel your life is leading to the goals you desire. That is why men and women have been able to push their bodies and minds to new limits; they felt what they were doing was worthwhile.

Live with your heart, and you'll have the energy to do everything you want to do.

In the process of sifting through the messages inside, you want to focus on a half-dozen or less. I am talking about important values such as truth, justice, compassion, kindness, health, honesty, integrity and creativity, to name some. As Robert Fritz says in his book, *The Path of Least Resistance*, this process changes you profoundly. "The standard of measurement in life shifts from emotional states to what is truly important and most worthy of you as a human being on this planet in this historic period. Your true satisfaction and fulfillment come from nothing short of this."

You do not have to be cautious and say to yourself that you will never achieve your dreams. Perhaps right now it is not clear to you how achieving your dream will look, but if it's based on a core value, something you believe in completely, you will achieve that dream if you set a goal to do so. Be careful! You will!

The simple truth is that we as human beings derive our greatest sense of satisfaction from our accomplishments. We can all accomplish what we want to accomplish in life. The hard part is figuring out what that is and then the rest is easy. This formula for achieving satisfaction is simple but don't be fooled by its simplicity. It is as powerful as a bomb exploding. This is how you do it.

The Beginning of Achievement

You decide what you want in life. Sift through all the garbage messages you've received about what you should want, what society says you should want, what you tell yourself you can do. Do you want to help other people? Do you want to achieve mastery in something? Do you want economic security? Do you want new and challenging experience? Do you want to realize your intellectual potential? These are the elementary choices you need to make upon which to build your life, the important values that truly matter to you.

Here are some values you will want to consider in the process of deciding your important values:

—achievement: a sense of accomplishment or mastery

—advancement: promotions

—adventure: new and challenging experiences

—affection: love, caring

—competitiveness: winning, taking risks

—cooperation: working well with others, teamwork

—creativity: being imaginative, innovative

—economic security: having enough money to pay the bills

—family happiness: a sense of well-being to you and your children and mate

—freedom: independence, autonomy, choices

—friendship: close relationships with others

—health: being physically well and active

—helpfulness: assisting others, improving society

—immortality: everlasting fame

—inner harmony: being at peace with yourself

—integrity: honesty, standing up for your beliefs

—involvement: participating with others, belonging

—loyalty: duty, obedience

—order: tranquility, stability, conformity

—personal development: use of potential

—pleasure: fun, laughs, a life with time for fun

—power: control, authority or influence over others

—recognition: respect from others, status

—religion: strong beliefs in God, practicing your faith

—responsibility: accountable for results

—self-respect: pride, sense of personal identity

—wealth: making money, getting rich

—wisdom: understanding life, discovering knowledge

Selecting your most important values is the foundation for developing your career plan. Your career plan will evolve from a process that flows from defining your values, setting goals based on your values, assessing what you already possess and where you need to develop, seeking information and resources to evaluate your plan, making career decisions, and then writing out a plan. In a flow chart format, the process looks like this:

Career Planning Process
◊
Values
◊
Goals
◊
Self-Assessment
◊
Resources/Information
◊
Evaluation
◊
Career Decision
◊
Career Plan

Setting Your Goals

The best way to overcome obstacles for gaining satisfactory employment is through realistic goal-oriented preparation.

If you decide you want to make more money, how are you going to make that money? Working for someone, or starting your own business? Do you have the necessary education, job experience, and resources to accomplish that objective? Figure out whatever you need to do to get whatever it is you want. Those are your goals. A goal is a desired achievement, a point which you wish to reach, an accomplishment, an outcome, or a prize you desire.

Goals fall into the categories of being immediate, short-term, or long-term. Immediate is what you must do now, today, this week. Short term is something you must do between one and three years. Long-term is something you do between three and five years from now.

You can have goals in many different areas of your life. They can be career-related, personal goals, financial goals, health goals, or family goals, to name different types of goals. For instance, a family goal might be to take a vacation to Yellowstone National Park. A financial goal might be to save up the down payment for a new car. A health goal might be to walk 20 minutes seven days a week.

Keep in mind that goals are reached in a step-by-step fashion. You will probably be working towards multiple goals at one time. You may modify your goals as time goes on. They're your goals; feel free to change them.

Also keep in mind that goal-setting is an on-going circular process. One goal may feed into another. If you decide you want to change jobs and make more money, you may begin a job search. You have an immediate goal of revising your resume and obtaining job interviews. In the search, you may learn that you need to enhance your skills further to reach your target goal of increased income. You decide you need to take some courses. You have a short-term goal. You may have to adjust your personal goals for awhile to make time for school. Later on, you may decide to go for a degree while working and you have a long term goal because it's going to take five years of schooling. Several years later, you may decide children are more important and take a break from school with the intention of picking school up again later. Feel free to modify and change your goals.

Self-Assessment

Now you need to go through a process of self-assessment. What do you already possess that will help you meet your goals? What do you need to obtain to achieve your goals? Skills are those abilities, talents, and competencies that have been acquired through personal living experiences as well as through on-the-job experiences. When you're ready, it may help to turn to the chapter on resumes near the end of the book and work through the resume writing worksheet to analyze your skills and abilities.

Interests and values are a good guide for direction setting in career choices. By tapping into your natural talents which are generally displayed in your interests, you can find career choices that tap into the things you want to succeed at. Because it is a natural match, you will be motivated to achieve because it is satisfying. Think back to the things you have done that have been so absorbing and rewarding that you worked on the tasks for hours without being aware of the passage of time or your body's needs. Those are the activities that will truly engage you and keep you motivated.

Do you like working with things? Working with people? Or working with data? No job is all one or the other, but jobs can be categorized generally into one of these three categories.

Verbs that describe working with things include: precision work, setting up, manipulating, controlling, operating, handling, tending, building. Jobs that deal primarily with things are, for example, auto mechanic, farmer, truck driver, painter, and seamstress. Working with things can be working with big things or little things, each different. Mechanics work with big things; a jeweler works with tiny parts and small tools. Look to your hobbies to see if this applies.

Do people give you energy? Do you like helping them or would your prefer to work alone? Working with people could be further broken down into working with large groups of people at a time, or working individually with people. A classroom teacher would be an example of someone working with groups of people whereas a medical doctor, though he/she sees hundreds of people a day, works with each of them individually, one at a time. Verbs that describe working with people include mentoring, negotiating, supervising, consulting, instructing, treating, coaching, persuading, helping, serving, exchanging information. Some job examples are teacher, counsellor, minister, receptionist, salesperson, union organizer, supervisor, to name a few.

Do you like working with data, information that contains facts and figures? If you like data, working with people can be an annoyance, but if you like people, working with data can be frustrating. Verbs that describe data jobs are analyzing, computing, compiling, counting, copying, and comparing. Jobs that deal primarily with data include software analyst, file clerk, bookkeeper, typist, proofreader, accountant, cashier, as examples.

There are other definite personality orientations which can also guide you in your career choices. Patterns for personalities are based on how we prefer to perceive information and how we prefer to make decisions based on that information.

You can perceive information about the world from the information from your senses. A sensory orientation is based on awareness of experience, good powers of observation and a memory for facts and details. Or you can get your information from the insight of intuition. Intuition is the act of knowing without the use of rational processes, a sixth sense, a hunch. Intuition provides the ability to see abstract, symbolic and theoretical relationships and deal with complexity. Our information-gathering orientation combined with how we make decisions creates a personality orientation.

If when you make a decision, you are analytical, and logical, sticking to the facts, you will come to a different conclusion than if you interact with the information personally, considering how you would feel, or how it impacts the individual. If you are a logical thinker combined with liking the facts based on the world around you, you would find your talents well used in technical fields with facts and objects as your goal.

If you prefer the facts from the world around you, but tend to be sympathetic and friendly about those facts, your talents might lie in health care, community service, sales, and teaching, where you could work with people.

If, on the other hand, you are intuitive and focus on possibilities and the overall picture, rather than details, combined with being logical and analytical in your approach to decisions, then going into theoretical and technical fields would draw upon your talents. Fields such as physical science, research, and management would be attractive to you. If, on the other hand, the possibilities and overall view are handled with the personal touch, you would probably find that you understand and communicate well with people. Therefore the fields of behavioral science, literature and the arts would be attractive to you and use your talents well.

Both your values and orientation should also guide you in making some selections within your choice categories. You should give some thought to what kind of work characteristics would suit you best. Do you like a small company which gives closer working relationships, and less defined duties? Or would you prefer a larger, more impersonal organization with clearly defined rules and procedures? Do you like to get up in the morning knowing what you'll do that day? Or is having the unexpected happen exciting? Do you like to travel? Do you like to take risks or would you prefer to avoid them? Does working at a fast pace with deadlines and pressure for results excite you and make you thrive, or do you want to go at a steady and sure pace? Do you like to work independently or have others dependent on your work? Do financial rewards tied to your work results motivate you or would you prefer to get a regular paycheck without the highs and lows of variable income? Do you like to work on short projects and then go on to something new or do you want to work at something that continues indefinitely? These work characteristics play a role in determining how satisfied you'll be with your job in addition to the work content. You might like the basic work content, but find that you're in the situation of how you perform the job that affects your satisfaction.

Resources/Information Gathering

This book should be just a beginning in your resource gathering. Read books, magazines, newspapers. Talk to people. Attend workshops and seminars sponsored by your community's colleges and technical schools. Make use of government information on jobs.

There is a wealth of written information available on careers. An excellent resource available in libraries, guidance offices, and at various public locations is the *Occupational Outlook Handbook*. It is published every two years by the U.S. Department of Labor. It describes over 250 occupations covering over one million jobs, or 86% of all jobs in the economy with emphasis on new or rapidly growing fields. Each occupational entry is two or three pages long and contains information on the nature of the work, places of employment, necessary qualifications and training, employment outlook (including the number of people now in the occupation and consideration of future prospects), earnings and working conditions, and sources of additional information. In addition, there is summary information on 80 occupations which account for another 5% of all jobs in the economy. By reviewing the book, you will gain a good overview of over 90% of the jobs available today.

Your personal contacts are also a good source of information. You can talk directly to people you know or know through other people who are doing something that looks interesting to you. By conducting an informational interview, you can find out what the job consists of, what kind of training is required, what a typical day consists of, and answers to many other questions.

Counselors are available in many different locations. Many of these services are free or inexpensive. Some of the locations where you might find a counselor include the high school guidance office, career planning and placement offices in colleges, placement offices in private/vocational/technical schools, vocational rehabilitation agencies, counseling services offered by community organizations, private counseling agencies or private practices, and state employment service offices affiliated with the U.S. Employment Service. Your personnel department at work should also be able to provide you with some career counseling.

A career counselor can administer different types of instruments that can guide you on career choice. One of these instruments is the Myers-Briggs Type Inventory which tells your personality orientation based on perception and judgment processes, i.e. how you gather information and make decisions. Your responses indicate your preferences and strengths. Another instrument is the Strong Interest Inventory. Based on your answers to many questions about your preferences, a computer printout suggests the kinds of occupations you are likely to prefer, the fields you should avoid, and the degree of similarity between your interest and those of employed people in many occupations. Another comprehensive tool is the "World of Work Inventory" by Hudson & Hudson. A printed profile is returned measuring your interests, abilities and work temperament on a continuum. There are many other types of instruments that I have not discussed.

An often overlooked source of information is professional societies, trade associations, labor unions, business firms, and educational institutions. By looking in the *Encyclopedia of Associations* (published by Gale Research Company) at the public library, you can write to these organizations and receive information on the types of jobs and careers that they represent.

While these resources are useful, any good career counselor, test or instrument can only guide you. Ultimately only you can answer the question of what you want to do, like to do, and find satisfying.

Choices Create Uncertainty

Even when you have made choices about what kind of work you like and how you like to do it, there is uncertainty. There are so many ways to fulfill some of your needs. Even when you know what those needs are, you might be able to do them in many different ways. It's similar to being in the middle of a maze and looking at dozens of possible ways to the end. A person who likes people could teach, work in a service industry or be a counselor.

Evaluation

In evaluation, you weigh all the information you have taken in about yourself and career options. Each potential career path has advantages and disadvantages. Only you can determine direction for your life. The evaluation process will take some time to complete, but in the end you will gain from a thorough understanding of who you are, what you want, and where you want to go.

Career Decisions

Finally you have to make a decision about which direction you will go. Don't let fear of making a wrong decision paralyze you into making no decision. No decision is a decision to continue to be passive, to continue just as you are. Reach out and take charge of your life. No one knows more about what is best for you than you. You are the expert on your life. Trust that you know best what is best for you.

Career Plan

Map out a career plan. Take your decision and decide what you need to do today, tomorrow, next week, next year to achieve your goals and write it down. Write down all the steps in the career planning process. Write down your values, goals, and career plan. It is essential that you write your career plan down.

Writing your career plan down gives it power because the plan then becomes concrete. You can read the words. Concrete ideas are more powerful than abstract ideas. By writing them down, they become concrete rather than mere thoughts in your head.

As is true in other areas of life, you only get what you ask for. When you write your career plan down, you are asking yourself to give yourself your dreams. This does something to your subconscious as well, giving the goals power in your mind.

Because they are written down, they are also measurable and you can assess your progress against them. You will make progress if you do these things and that progress will make you feel good, satisfied, and give you the momentum to keep going. Nothing succeeds like success. When you see your success, you will strive for further success because you will feel so good about your accomplishments.

When you write your plan down, the plan also guides you in the many decisions you will make on the use of your time. There is too much to do in life. We need priorities to guide us on what we want to be doing. The fundamental choices you have made, your values, will determine your priorities. If raising happy confident children is important, maybe you'll forego an activity that is purely for your pleasure, and pick a family activity instead. If using your intellectual potential is a primary value, maybe you'd choose to go to school rather than be a volunteer in the community.

Nibbling Away At Your Goals

When you are advancing on your plan, keep in mind that the Swiss cheese effect works. You can nibble away at your goals; they don't have to be accomplished in one fell swoop.

Achieving Goals Should Give Satisfaction

Goals are important because achieving them gives you satisfaction. In the process of setting and achieving your goals, don't forget that the process of achieving goals is your life. Everything you do should be pleasurable to you at some level and you should enjoy the process. Working to achieve goals is part of the secret; enjoying the process of achieving goals is the other part of the secret.

There is a parable by Robert J. Hastings, called "The Station", which captures this concept. I'd like to share it with you:

> Tucked away in our subconscious is an idyllic vision. We see ourselves on a long trip that spans the continent. We are traveling by train. Out the windows we drink in the passing scene of cars on nearby highways, of children waving at a crossing, of cattle grazing on a distant hillside, of smoke pouring from a power plant, of row upon row of corn and wheat, of flatlands and valleys, of mountains and rolling hillsides, of city skylines and village halls.
>
> But uppermost in our minds is the final destination. On a certain day at a certain hour we will pull into the station. Bands will be playing and flags waving. Once we get there so many wonderful dreams will come true and the pieces of our lives will fit together like a completed jigsaw puzzle. How restlessly we pace the aisles, damning

> the minutes for loitering—waiting, waiting, waiting for the station.
>
> 'When we reach the station, that will be it!' we cry. 'When I'm 18.' 'When I buy a new 450 SL Mercedes Benz!' 'When I put the last kid through college.' 'When I have paid off the mortgage!' 'When I get a promotion.' 'When I reach the age of retirement, I shall live happily every after!'
>
> Sooner or later, we must realize there is no station, no one place to arrive at once and for all. The true joy of life is the trip. The station is only a dream. It constantly outdistances us.
>
> 'Relish the moment' is a good motto, especially when coupled with Psalm 118:24: 'This is the day which the Lord hath made: we will rejoice and be glad in it.' It isn't the burdens of today that drive men (sic) mad. It is the regrets over yesterday and the fear of tomorrow. Regret and fear are twin thieves who rob us of today.
>
> So stop pacing the aisles and counting the miles. Instead, climb more mountains, eat more ice cream, go barefoot more often, swim more rivers, watch more sunsets, laugh more, cry less. Life must be lived as we go along. The station will come soon enough.

Samuel Johnson also said it, but shorter, "The process is the reality." As you strive for your goals, enjoy, savor, appreciate your life as much as possible. Focus on the now, the today, and all your tomorrows will take care of themselves.

As Fritz says in his book:

> The more you realize that what you truly want really matters the more selective you become about what you want. You recognize the importance of your deepest wants and less important ones take a secondary place.

> As you reunite with your power to create, most likely you will discover that what truly matters to you is worthy of you — for example, health, freedom, justice, and being true to yourself.

Setting and achieving goals will make you feel worthy of your humanity and help you overcome any previously perceived shortcomings. It is so simple, yet so few take the time or make the effort to do it. By doing it for yourself, you will experience satisfaction; you will contribute your creative power to the world. The old saying, "Nothing succeeds like success," is accurate. Once you experience the personal power that comes from achieving your dreams, you will not want to go back to living any other way. You will feel successful. You will be successful. You are doing what you want to do.

RECOMMENDATIONS FOR FURTHER WORK

1. Take time to dream. Dream your dreams. Then figure out how you'll reach them.
2. Write down your values. Use the list in this chapter to help decide what they are. Go through and pick ten values on your first pass. Go back and narrow it down to five. Write those down. Then write down your goals based on the values. Make an immediate, short, and long range plan. Immediate is what you must do now. Short-term is what you want to accomplish between one and three years from today. Long-range is 3 to 5 years.
3. Don't be afraid to revise your list. It's your list! As you get into the process, you'll catch the spirit!

Chapter Three

Learning Opportunities

In today's fast-paced, ever-changing world, learning is a fundamental ingredient to a successful work place career. In fact, if you analyze it, learning is the key to a happy, successful life. We learn constantly in order to advance ourselves to higher levels of accomplishments in all areas of life. We learn new skills and knowledge which make life more enjoyable and provide us with satisfying experiences. We learn the fundamentals as children so that we can go on to learn even more exciting information about the world around us. We learn how to get along with people in general, make friends, find a partner, keep a marriage together. We learn how to take care of a baby, then a toddler, then a child, adjust to having teenagers, and finally to having adult children. We learn how to knit, ride a bicycle, play tennis, ski, sail a boat, fish so that we can more fully enjoy our bodies, the outdoors, and life. These are just a few of the thousands of things we learn in order to be fully alive and successful human beings. Why should working be any different?

We learn basic skills first, then more skills and knowledge to advance to new and challenging work experiences.

People confuse learning with formal education. Formal learning opportunities may provide a portion of our learning experiences but we learn constantly in many different ways.

We learn by reading, watching others, and trial and error. Perhaps we get a better start when the foundation to our learning is organized and structured so that we learn the most vital facts first, and a framework in which to fill in our facts. People who think of learning as associated with just a high school, college, or a technical school education are limiting themselves by not using all the different learning vehicles available. Some of these vehicles may actually be better methods of learning for your unique situation. While formal vehicles of learning are important, the variety of learning opportunities available to you is tremendous. Consider this list of some of the educational opportunities available to you:

—Advanced college programs
—4-year traditional college programs
—Non-traditional college programs such as independent study, recognition for experience, credit by examination
—Special classroom training
—Part-time attendance at school
—Apprenticeships
—Armed Forces training (Army, Navy, Air Force, Marines, and Coast Guard, National Guard)
—Government training programs
—Hospital schools
—G. E. D.
—On-the-job experience
—Observation of someone skilled
—Mentoring
—Two-year community or vocational education
—Special training courses offered by industry
—On-the-job training
—Videotapes and cassette tapes

—Employment-related seminars
—College courses for professional growth and development
—Private schools
—Correspondence courses
—Reading on the topic
—High school diploma

The list shows a range from the most advanced to a high school diploma. There are formal organized learning experiences on the list and informal methods on the list. There are things you can do on your own, such as reading or listening to tapes, and things you need to do with other people, such as attend a class. The list does not include every method of learning. There are other ways to learn that are not included.

Earnings and Learning

Roughly half of the difference in earnings in the U.S. can be explained by differences in learning in school and on the job. The other half of the difference in earnings is explained by geography, career choice, and the selection of an employer. Earnings therefore are a function of the skills you possess and the choices you make regarding how and where you use your skills.

If you have a good foundation of basic skills, you will be able to expand and grow those skills on the job. This will allow you to leverage those skills to get a better job.

Naturally earnings also go up with the increase in education. With eight years of school or less, the median annual earnings of fulltime female workers is $10,088. With one to three years of high school the median earnings increase to $11,815. With four years of high school the median annual earnings increase to $14,698, and with one to three years of college, they increase to $16,724. With four or more years of college, they increase to $23,276.[1] The more education you have, the more you earn on the job.

However, the American Society of Training and Development says that formal education accounts for only a 15 percent variation in lifetime earnings, compared to 85 percent generated by work place learning. Training provides most skills acquired after age 25 and all skills for two out of three jobs. Individuals with a high school diploma and two years of formal education have a 20 percent greater chance of receiving on-the-job training than individuals with only a high school diploma. Individuals with some college education have an even greater chance of getting on-the-job training, a 50 percent greater chance. On-the-job learning, especially formal learning, can also increase earnings, by as much as 30 percent.[2]

Why You Need Basic Skills as a Minimum

The work place is changing dramatically. Businesses are struggling to remain competitive on a worldwide basis. Swift technical changes are occurring in the way work is done. Companies need to bring their products to market quickly. The need to provide excellent customer service is a requirement to remain competitive. All these changes affect the role the worker plays. Each employee plays an important role in a company's success. New business strategies are being put into place to help companies remain competitive and produce higher quality products. These strategies mean that team concepts, total quality management, and the ability to use computers are making even entry level jobs complicated. Most employers are now seeing that every employee directly affects the bottom line of the corporation and they are investing in their employees at unprecedented levels.

Employers are also realizing that they can no longer rely on a strategy of replacement to get the workers they need. American employers are faced with a reduced pool of effectively skilled workers. For the first time, the 16-24 year old age group that traditionally supplied new entry-level workers is shrinking demographically. Employers now have to invest in their employees to an extent not previously seen in order to have access to the necessary skilled workers.

American business is currently spending $210 billion for on-the-job training, about equal to all the nation's public education combined. Employee training by employers is the largest delivery system for adult education and will probably grow in the decade ahead.

What Are the Work Place Basics?

The American Society of Training and Development and the U.S. Department of Labor Employment and Training Administration conducted a two year study of the skills needed by American employers. While employers are using the study as a model to set up work place training programs, individuals can also benefit from the study by using it as a blueprint to guide them in up-skilling themselves to meet the challenges in today's work place. Here is the study's list of skills needed by employers:

- Learning to Learn
- 3 R's (Reading, Writing, Computation)
- Communication: Listening and Oral
- Creative Thinking/Problem Solving
- Personal Management: Self-Esteem, Goal Setting, Motivation, and Career Development
- Interpersonal, Negotiation, and Teamwork Skills
- Organizational Effectiveness/Leadership Skills

Let's look at each of these skills to understand what they are comprised of, why they are important, and how you can obtain these basics.

Learning to Learn

This is the most basic of all skills. Knowing how to learn will enable you to achieve competency in all the other work place skills. Understanding how you best learn—through visual, auditory, or tactile stimulation—and actively pursuing a strategy to provide you with the best approach that works for you will allow you to dramatically improve your rate of learning.

Visual learners learn best when they can see a picture in their minds. Auditory learners learn mainly through their ears. They may be able to tell the answer without being able to write it down. Tactile learners learn through their bodies. When they have to sit still, their brains seem to go to sleep.

If you are a visual learner, seeing the information that you are trying to absorb written down will help you. Write out the procedure you are trying to understand. Make lists of the information you are trying to memorize. Watch a video if possible, and read the information you need to absorb.

If you are an auditory learner, memory cues connected with rhymes or poems will help. Repeating out loud what you are trying to learn will help.

If you are a tactile learner, moving around while you are learning helps, even standing up may improve your ability to absorb the information. Use a finger to focus your eyes on the information you are reading, or act out a procedure to help you remember it better. These strategies will help you incorporate a learning method that will help you learn new information.

3 R's (Reading, Writing, Computation)

Computers have invaded the work place. Statistical process control has been introduced to improve product quality. Writing to communicate with customers, document procedures, or communicate with others is now more important than ever.

Algebra is now needed to track production quality using Statistical Process Control techniques.

Jobs today no longer have workers simply placing a part in the manufacturing process or using regular process or repetitive interaction with production equipment. Reading and writing, documentation of procedures, computing production statistics, and following diagrams and computer procedures are a part of most jobs. Today, 38.3% of the workforce uses computers on the job in word processing, bookkeeping, inventory control, communications, and databases. The percentage is even higher for women: 46% of the female workforce use a computer.[4]

Workers spend an average of one and one-half to two hours per work day engaged in reading various things such as forms, charts, graphs, manuals, computer terminals, etc. Writing remains the primary form of communication in a work setting. Computation is used daily to conduct inventories, report on production levels, measure machine parts or specifications, and so on.

If you don't have the basics in reading, writing, and arithmetic, you need to get them. You will not be able to advance on the job, perhaps even retain your current job, without these fundamentals. If you don't have a high school diploma, you can earn one through an alternative high school program, such as a G.E.D. program through the technical college in your community or an alternative high school through your public school system. If you do have a high school diploma, and you feel your skills in reading, writing, and computation are still weak, you can take courses through your technical school, junior college, or local college for credit towards a degree or non-credit to improve your skills in the 3R's. There are many opportunities all around you to improve these skills.

Communication: Listening and Oral

The average person spends 55% of their communication time listening; 23% speaking; 13.3% reading and 8.4% writing.[5] Only job knowledge ranks in higher terms in success factors. Yet few employees have received formal training in how to communicate effectively by listening well or speaking well. Understanding the importance of voice inflection, body language, the styles that people use when communicating and how they affect how they are perceived and what is heard makes you a more effective worker. Learning the five listening skills—listening for content, listening to conversations, listening for long-term contexts, listening for emotional meaning, and listening to follow directions—will make you understand how listening style affects the sending and receiving of information and will make you a more effective worker.

Courses are available in communications. You can take them for credit or non-credit at community colleges, vocational schools, and universities. You can also learn communications by listening to cassette tapes, watching videotapes on the subject, reading books. You can attend leadership and communications training sponsored by community, volunteer, and church groups. Oftentimes these sessions are provided to improve their group leaders but the skills are transferable to all areas of life. All of us can benefit from improving our skills in these areas.

Creative Thinking/Problem Solving

Problem solving skills include the ability to recognize and define problems, come up with solutions and select the most effective solution and track its effectiveness. Creative thinking, or the ability to see problems in new ways results in new and better solutions to existing problems. The ability to solve problems creatively and implement the solutions enables workers to progress in an organization.

Organizations are putting in place quality improvement programs that depend on workers' ability to define problems and solve them creatively. Manufacturing processes need to be continually refined to accomplish their task more efficiently and effectively. All employees are being called on to help improve the work place. Fundamental to that is an employee's ability to deal with problems and think creatively about their solutions.

Again, courses are available which deal with problem-solving. Books are available on the topic. A basic course or book will help you understand that problem-solving is a process that can be analyzed. By understanding the process—defining the problem, looking for solutions creatively, and selecting the solution that seems to work best—we can all improve our ability to solve problems.

Personal Management: Self Esteem, Goal Setting, Motivation, and Career Development

Employers are beginning to recognize that confident employees who have a good self-image take pride in their work, and are able to motivate themselves to achieve their best on the job and pursue company as well as personal goals. A self-confident employee has a career plan and is willing to work to achieve success in the work place. The employee is being proactive, not reactive, about their future.

Up until recently, self-esteem and motivation were not considerations in hiring. Employers looked at skills and knowledge as the primary qualifications for hiring. Employers now understand that a self-confident employee is aware of their current skill level and has personal goals to learn new skills. An employee with good self-esteem has self-awareness and understands how they impact others, what is stressful to them, and works at developing qualities that help them cope in a rapidly changing work place.

Obviously you possess a desire to develop good personal management or you would not be reading this book. Pursue your desire to be in charge of your life and develop a career plan.

Interpersonal, Negotiation, and Teamwork Skills

Teamwork has become extremely important in the work place. Employers recognize that through teamwork, high product quality and higher productivity result. Employers are now seeking employees who can work together as members of a team and pull together to achieve common goals. Working successfully as part of team requires effective interpersonal skills, negotiation skills and teamwork skills. This means team members need to learn how to deal with different types of people, understand group dynamics, understand how to give feedback to co-workers and receive feedback from others. They must be able to recognize the valuable differences of others and how to use each team member as effectively as possible to achieve the common goal.

The worker who cannot be a successful team member will find that there is no place for the lone ranger in today's organization.

If you are employed, chances are your employer is emphasizing teamwork. Take advantage of the courses and training offered. Pursue training offered at local educational institutions and set personal goals to practice your skills.

Organizational Effectiveness/Leadership

Employers now recognize that everyone on the payroll has to be a leader. Every employee has to understand that each company is an organization with its own culture and own set of rules. When the employee recognizes these realities, innocence of company politics is replaced by a greater understanding of how to effectively achieve results and get things done in the organization's unique culture. With these qualities, any employee can become a master problem-solver, an innovator and a team builder. This means each employee has some power to influence others to get things done in a certain way.

Observe employees who are effective leaders and try to model their behavior. Learn to think for yourself and talk about your ideas.

Other Learning Strategies

If you are employed, your employer may offer courses in any of those topics, and you should take advantage of those courses. Let your supervisor know you want to improve, what you want to take, and work with the supervisor to come up with your own development plan. Many companies also have their own internal training departments, and administrators of those training programs who can also offer you guidance and help in developing a strategy.

You also may be surprised at the wealth of learning resources that can help you in all the basic skill areas without doing so directly. A parenting effectiveness course, for example, not only helps you become a better parent, but helps you communicate more effectively with everyone in your life, solve conflict, and set goals. A church activity can provide you with valuable leadership practice, and may even offer leadership training. All you need to do is transfer the leadership skills from church to work. Girl Scouts, women's groups, community groups offer training for their leaders which is valuable training for all areas of your life.

Another learning strategy is to be a better TV viewer. Many credit and non-credit courses in these areas are offered through your local and state schools on TV. Watching business programs where industry leaders are interviewed or discussed can also give you valuable insight into how organizations function, and how leaders operate. It can greatly increase your understanding of what kind of environment your company is functioning in and the challenges it faces.

Take Charge Now!

If you don't have basic skills, you are not going to get very far on the job. The price of ignorance will be low-paying jobs lasting a lifetime. Even if you have the basics, if you don't continue to learn, the price of your standing still will be continuing low pay, lack of advancement, or no job at all! Take charge today; don't say it's too late. It's never too late to become something more than you are today and the benefits will be returned in more challenging job duties, higher pay, and greater satisfaction with your work life.

Be Pragmatic if You Have To

The opportunity to learn is always there. It is always possible to learn by enrolling in a program of study, even if it was a missed opportunity for you at some other point in your life. If you didn't get a high school diploma at the age of 18 because you dropped out of school, you can obtain its equivalent through a G.E.D. program, attend alternative high school, or get accepted into a college by passing a test. If you choose not to attend a two or four year college because you work fulltime or have a family to raise, you can still choose to take advantage of education and take one course at a time. Sooner or later, those individual courses will add up to an impressive list of courses. You can obtain specialized training in other ways, for example by joining the military, or getting accepted into an apprenticeship program. If you have some college, you can augment your education with other college courses without the intention of finishing your degree, or you can have a degree, and decide to take additional courses to develop a better understanding in areas you didn't previously study.

Education does not have to proceed in a lock-step fashion in order to bring the results you desire. A pragmatic approach is especially useful to non-traditional students, those who are not fitting the pattern of other students. A pragmatic approach is far better than doing nothing because the task seems overwhelming. Nibbling at the goal will create opportunities for you. Some training or education is always better than none.

You can benefit by not locking yourself into a preconceived notion of what is the right way to learn. The right way to learn is the way that works for you when you are ready to learn and brings you the satisfaction and rewards you are seeking.

Because employers are now more aware than ever before that they have to develop the basic skills of their employees to remain competitive, you will benefit. Simply having an awareness of what skills you already possess, where you need to improve, and a desire to do so will get you moving. Being motivated to grow will make you aware of the many opportunities offered to do so and actively participating in these opportunities will help you get the most out of them.

Make a Development Plan for Yourself

Each person needs to have a development plan for themselves. You must be in charge to make changes happen in your work life . No one else can do it or cares enough to do it for you. A development plan is a subset of your career plan. A development plan defines the learning that needs to occur in order for you to advance your skill and knowledge level. Your development plan can consist of many different learning strategies: taking classes, reading books, participating in on-the-job training offered by your employer, participating in a new work activity, or setting a personal goal to improve your work methods on your own. Whatever works for you will result in improvement.

The ground under your feet is constantly moving and you must continue to keep up or you will be left behind. If you aspire to having a decent standard of living, you simply have to get on the learning track to keep a toehold with employers' rising expectations and changing job requirements.

If you believe that you can learn — and you can, of course— the battle is half won. Get going on a plan to help you learn what you want to learn. You will discover your potential is much greater than you ever dreamed possible.

RECOMMENDATIONS FOR FURTHER WORK

1. Pick a learning goal, something you have always wanted to learn to do and set a date for beginning and ending. You will begin to see how easy it is to accomplish something important to you.
2. If you are employed, visit your personnel department and ask to see job descriptions of positions you might want to work towards to find out what you need to learn and do to achieve a better job.
3. If you are not employed, call the career planning center at your local technical college or university to see what kind of guidance services they offer at no charge. Then make an appointment to take advantage of these services.

[1]Taeuber, Cynthia. *Statistical Handbook on Women in America.* Phoenix, Arizona: Oryx Press, 1991, p. 99.
[2]Carnevale, Anthony P. and Leila J. Gainer and Ann S. Meltzer. *Workplace Basics: The Skills Employers Want.* The American Society for Training and Development and The U.S. Department of Labor, Employment and Training Administration.
[3]US Bureau of the Census, *Statistical Abstract of the United States: 1991 (111th Edition.)* Washington, DC 1991, p. 412.
[4]Carnevale, Anthony, p. 11
[5]Ibid, p. 5.

Chapter Four

Non-Traditional Careers

Traditionally women have held jobs in the clerical, service, or menial categories, where they have dominated those occupations. 98.3% of the secretaries are female; 97.3% of receptionists are female; 92.9% of telephone operators are female; 96.6% of typists are female. Other occupations dominated by women at this level include: key punch operators, dental assistants, registered nurses, practical nurses, waitresses, bank tellers, filing clerks, bookkeepers, cashiers and file clerks.

Yet there is a whole world of trades and occupations which could be exciting and satisfying careers where women make up the minority. A non-traditional career field has recently been defined by federal legislation passed in late 1991 as an occupation or field of work where women comprise less than 25 percent of the individuals employed in the occupation or field of work.

Many of these occupations or fields require two years or less of formal training, or an apprenticeship or company provided training program. Why aren't women considering these fields? Why don't you become one of the pioneers and break old barriers?

Are You Interested? Could You Do It?

These skills and trades are different from anything you might have considered in the past. These skills and trades might satisfy you far more than one of the traditional occupations could. But they require that you work in settings that are sometimes dirty, noisy, and demanding physically. Ask yourself:

—Can I work where I'd be exposed to constant contact with mud, dust, sparks, grease, dirt, or other unclean working conditions?

—Can I stand a high level of noise at the job site?

—Am I allergic to any of the substances used on the job?

—Can I work at heights?

—Can I work outdoors in all kinds of weather?

—Would I object to shift work?

—Would I be willing to undertake physical training to qualify for a job?

Possible Trades or Skills To Consider

If you answered yes to most of these questions, perhaps you should consider a non-traditional type of job or skill in your future. Here is a teaser list of the many different non-traditional occupations for women available in today's working world:

radio and TV announcers
insurance sales workers
utility meter readers
fire fighters
construction carpenter
stonemason
glazier
painter
cable splicer
telephone line installer
telephone installer
broadcast technician
television camera operator
air conditioning mechanic
refrigeration mechanic
heating mechanic
air craft mechanic
automotive mechanic
boiler tender
building custodian
electronic technician
locksmith
corrections officers and jailers
sheriffs and deputy sheriffs
fish and game wardens
butchers and meat cutters
barbers
log handling equipment operators
forest and conservation workers
log graders and scalers
machinery maintenance workers
motorcycle repairers
mobile home repairers
coin and vending machine servicers

bicycle repairers
reinforcing metal workers
pipe layers
septic tank and sewer operators
air hammer operators
paving, surfacing, and tamping workers
highway maintenance workers
sheet metal duct installers
cabinetmakers and bench carpenters
slaughterers and butchers
welding machine operators
printing press machine operators
water and waste treatment plant operators
heavy or tractor trailer truck drivers
light and delivery truck operators
taxi drivers and chauffeurs
ship, boat and barge mates
hoist and winch operators
crane and tower operators
operating engineers
mechanic and repairer helpers

A non-traditional job is not for every woman but a non-traditional job may fit better for you than the traditional occupations. You should consider your interest in the skills and trades. If you're interested, work out a plan to get trained and employed in a field you might have never dreamed you would work in. Women like you will make it possible for other women to consider their options in the skills and trade fields as well.

RECOMMENDATIONS FOR FURTHER WORK

1. Contact your local vocational/technical school for more information on the training they provide in some of these fields. Many schools have special grants which provide training to

women in non-traditional occupations. The grant may reimburse participants for travel and child care expenses.

2. Contact the state apprenticeship office and find out how you could get considered for an apprenticeship. An apprenticeship program integrates training with work so you are getting the learning you need while earning a living.

3. Check out the training programs offered in the Armed Forces. Their programs will train you for some of these occupations.

4. Employers are always looking for women in fields where there are few. It helps them achieve their Affirmative Action/ Equal Employment Opportunity Goals. Contact your local employers and find out where they need women to help them achieve equal employment and what their qualification requirements are.

Chapter Five

Be Your Own Boss!

Become an entrepreneur! Being in business for yourself has never looked better! Self-employment provides women with the flexibility they need to balance their lives. 4.5 million businesses in the U.S. are owned by women. A self-employed woman may be able to run the business out of her home. She can determine her own hours. She can build on a strong interest or the natural tendency to be a service provider. She can be creative. There are no limits to the earning potential, and even though the risks and chances for failure are high, the satisfaction is also great. Furthermore, with women still earning on average 68% of what males earn, the difficulties of competing in an office or factory setting with males are eliminated. Owning a small business is hard work and requires business skills and a plan. The free market has formidable challenges, but even with these challenges, those with the energy, enthusiasm, persistence and skills can succeed and achieve their personal dreams.

There are different ways of becoming a business owner. You can start a business from scratch and go it alone or form a partnership or corporation. You can purchase an established business. You can buy a franchise. All offer advantages and disadvantages. You will have to develop a business plan and then select an option which you feel will best meet your objectives and uses your business skills.

The decade of the 80's was the decade of small businesses. Small business-dominated industries like restaurants, bars, and services grew more in employment than large business dominated industries. Proprietorship earnings grew at a higher rate than corporate profits and salaries. Throughout the 1980's, small businesses have been growing faster, reacting more quickly, and have been economically more productive than large businesses.[1]

But the reality is four out of five new businesses fail within the first five years. This is primarily because of undercapitalization. The demands placed on small business owners include long and irregular hours during the start-up phase, stresses placed on family relationships as a result of the owner's involvement, and lack of benefits and other perks that come from steady employment.

However, for women, the picture looks brighter. The American Home Business Association is predicting that home-based businesses will increase by 33 percent between now and the mid-1990's. Niches created by our culture's new life styles are ripe for women to develop into businesses. Women entrepreneurs tend toward service and such businesses are relatively cheap to launch. Some statistics indicate that fewer than one in four female businesses failed, compared with four out of five of all U.S. businesses.

Have You Got What It Takes ?

When starting a small business, you are facing a long-term commitment. You should consider these factors affecting you and your business over the long term. Some of these include:

—Are you willing to work hard, not just from nine to five Monday through Friday, but up to 70 hours a week in the early months of making your business successful?

—How will your business affect your family life? Are they supportive of your venture?

—How well do your personal expectations correspond to the realities of operating a business in your chosen field?

—If you plan to form a partnership, are your prepared to share decision making?

—If you plan to work for yourself, are your prepared to go it alone?

—Are you willing to take the financial and personal risks involved?

—Is your health good so that you can meet the demands of your business?

—Are you willing to do whatever it takes to be successful, from sweeping floors to keeping books?

—Are you courageous and brave?

—Do you have common sense and above average intelligence?

—Do you have a sense of urgency about getting started?

—Does your business idea excite you and make you feel creative?

—Is there a real market for the product or service?

—Can you access the market?

—Is your product or service competitive with others?

—Is the risk manageable. Can you personally survive its failure?

—Is the cash flow from operations adequate?

—Can you obtain the professional and technical assistance when necessary?

—Is there a realistic need for this business?

—Do you have adequate knowledge to conduct the business and and its management?

—Can you work well with customers?

If you answered yes to these questions, you may have the ideas and drive you need to succeed.

Basis of Ideas for Business

Basically there are three kinds of ideas that are the basis for all business. The first is an idea that addresses an existing need that has previously gone unsatisfied. A bookstore that sells only cookbooks is an example of an idea that didn't exist until a couple in New York decided to open a book store that focused just on cookbooks.

The second is something that addresses an existing need better than any of the alternatives. A woman of German heritage took her recipe for pretzels and marketed the product to local businesses which agreed to let her bring them in for purchase by employees on their break. The homemade pretzel satisfied a need for a mid-morning snack that was healthier than the doughnuts and sweet rolls that are traditional in an office. She brought them in only one morning a week thereby continuing the specialness of the treat.

The third basis is for something so revolutionary that it creates its own need. A good example of that is the VCR. Ten years ago, few owned a VCR or dreamed they would need one to tape or show movies or TV programs. Today more than sixty percent of American households own a VCR.

Organizing an Independent Business

If you decide to organize a business from scratch, you should prepare a clear plan that takes your idea and shapes it into a profit-making business. Your business plan is probably your biggest key to success. Studies show that businesses with a written business plan are more likely to succeed than those operating without one. The major reasons for business failure are undercapitalization and lack of management skills. A well written business plan will help you spot potential problems.

Starting your own business is a big undertaking. You should not begin this venture without advisors. There are many free resources to help small businesses get a good start because small business plays such a big role in the prosperity of the U.S. These include the federal and state Small Business Administration offices which offers free advice to start-up companies through different agencies. The vocational and technical schools also offer many courses in entrepreneurship and business skills needed by small businesses. Many states and local communities have set up incubation and development centers to advise and assist small businesses in the beginning years. The organizations SCORE (Service Core of Retired Executives) and Ace (Active Corps of Executives) are programs established by the U.S. Small Business Administration to help all types of small businesses gain access to business consulting from experienced business operators and executives. Your local chamber of commerce is also a source of help.

Legal Forms of Organization

There are three legal forms of organizing your business: sole proprietorship, partnerships, and corporations. Each form has its own advantages and disadvantages. While it is possible for a business to start under one structure and change to another later, proper planning can prevent difficulties caused by an unsuitable form of organization.

Sole proprietorships are the most common form of business organization. A sole proprietorship is an unincorporated business owned by a single individual. Advantages of sole proprietorship include freedom of operation and the least amount of paperwork if no employees are involved. The owner is personally responsible for all obligations, debts, income taxes, and other liabilities for the business.

A partnership is one or more individuals and businesses operating as co-owners under a business agreement. The agreement should be in writing. It states the powers, liabilities, and authority of each partner. Outside advisors such as accountants and lawyers should be consulted when the partnership agreement is drawn up because partnership is a complicated matter which has long lasting implications. These advisors can prevent legal, financial or operating problems down the road.

Corporations are another form of business ownership. A corporation is a legally created entity distinct from its owners with rights, duties, powers, and responsibilities in and of itself. This usually means that when individuals act on behalf of a corporation,these actions are attributable to the corporation, not the individual. The advantage of a corporation is that liability is limited and other individuals can be brought into the business to raise capital. The corporation also continues to exist after the death or withdrawal of one owner. There is more than one form of corporation. The Subchapter S corporation combines the advantages of the partnership with the advantages of a corporation yet avoids double taxation by having its income taxed to the shareholders as if the corporation were a partnership. Again, outside advice from lawyers and accountants should definitely be sought if you incorporate your business.

Franchising: An Alternative to Starting Your Own Business

Franchising is a method of doing business where a parent company, the franchisor, grants an individual outlet owner, the franchisee, the right to market its products and services while using the franchisor's proven name, reputation, and marketing techniques. The franchisor will assist is selecting a business site, help negotiate a lease, help hire and train staff, outfit the site, establish supply lines and generally set the franchisee up in business. In return for these services, the franchise pays a front-end fee and on-going percentage of gross sales, usually 4-8% of gross sales.

$10 out of every $100 that the average consumer spends at the retail level is spent in a franchised establishment. Employment in franchising totals 7.2 million part and fulltime employees. The failure rate for franchised businesses is also much smaller than independent businesses.[2]

Comparative Success Rate
Franchised Businesses vs. Independent Businesses[3]

	Franchised	Independent Businesses
After 1st Year	97%	62%
After 5th Year	92%	23%
After 10th Year	90%	18%

The advantages to franchising are many. The business has been tested and you are buying a known product or service. There is a track record of financial and marketing success. There is expert help available in merchandising, inventory, location selection, accounting practices, and advertising programs you can tap. The disadvantage is that you owe a continuing percentage of gross sales in return for these advantages and can develop your business only to the extent that your franchise agreement allows.

Franchising is becoming one of the most popular methods of starting a business today. If you decide to investigate this possibility, you have a lot of homework to do, first to narrow down what type of business you might be interested in and then to select a suitable franchisor.

Buying an Existing Business: Another Alternative

Another alternative to starting your own business is to purchase an on-going, existing business. This can be less risky because the enterprise has been proven and you will realize a profit quicker from your investment. The business has a proven track record, location, equipment, inventory, customer base and staff. But you have to keep in mind that the seller is selling for a reason. You need to investigate very carefully to be sure you are not buying a failing business or that the location is bad, equipment outdated, customers unhappy, and staff disgruntled.

Information is available to help you determine a fair purchase price, based on different methods of valuing the business. Again, you should seek help in considering this alternative. An accountant and attorney are definitely necessary to help you consider the feasibility of this idea and to avoid legal, financial and operating difficulties later on.

Other Business Opportunities

There are other business opportunities that do not fall into the category of franchising or buying an existing business. These include dealerships, license agreements and distributorships. These arrangements allow greater freedom than franchises because the owners can run them as they see fit. Some have on-going support systems and others are one-time purchases.

A licensee pays for the right to sell a company's product or use a company's name. A distributor sells a company's products but doesn't use the company's name as its own. A rack jobber buys a route from a company entitling them to restock products on store shelves along a specified route.

There is less federal regulation so careful investigation is necessary to make a wise decision. Examples of business opportunities run a wide range: from computer portrait systems to hot tubs, from mini-golf courses to environmentally friendly products, from security systems to instant signs. The investment is often less than other business investments, as little as $200 or thousands of dollars.

These Ideas Are Just a Starting Point

The whole point of this chapter is to simply raise the question for your consideration: would owning a business be something you might want to do? If you answer yes, you have work ahead of you before you are ready to act on the idea. You might need to gain education, training, business skills, and work in a small business firsthand to see what it's like. Millions of women have become business owners and with great success. But go into the idea with your eyes open. It's hard work and there is no guarantee of success. On the other hand, it might be the most exciting satisfying avenue open to you. If you don't consider it, you haven't considered all the alternatives available to you at this point in your life.

RECOMMENDATIONS FOR FURTHER WORK

1. For the fun of it, brainstorm a list of business ideas you might consider if you started your own business.
2. Check out a book from the library that deals with starting your own business.
3. Talk to your friends that are in business for themselves and find out how they got started. Find out what challenges they face and what kind of satisfaction they derive from being in business for themselves.

[1] Pollan, Stephen M. and Mark Levine. *The Field Guide to Starting a Business.* New York: Fireside Books, Simon and Schuster, Inc., 1990.
[2] Bond, Robert E. and Christoper E. Bond. *The Source Book of Franchise Opportunities.* Irwin, Inc.: Homewood, Il, 1992.
[3] Ibid.

Chapter Six

Capitalizing on Trends

What are some of the changes in the world that are affecting job opportunities for today and tomorrow?

Aging Population

One trend is that the general population is growing older. As the average age moves upward, the population requires more health services to meet the shift. Health care will boom as old age creeps up on the population and the need for services from physical therapists, nurses, pharmacists, to name just a few professions, will increase. We will also see geographical areas where demand for these services is greater than the average national demand because retirees tend to cluster in certain states and areas.

Shifting Demographics

There is a decline in the number of young people. Demographics already tell us that there is a reduction in the number of workers entering the labor pool. This demographic change creates several implications for change. Employers have to reach to the labor pools of minorities and women to find the workers they need. They have to train those workers to do the job and they will have to promote them into positions of increased responsibility. This means more training to do the job of the future will be provided by employers. This is exciting for women and minorities. We may finally see true equal treatment.

Programs for Families

Because more women are working than ever before, we will probably see more programs to help women stay in the work place, such as child care programs and sick child care assistance. Some fast food chains are having so much trouble recruiting teenagers that they provide mothers with flexible work schedules, such as time off in the summer, and work shifts that coincide with the school day, to keep women in the work place. We will probably also see more employer-provided programs to help the middle-aged deal with their aging parents. Employers are beginning to see the baby boomers squeezed by their child-raising and parent-helping responsibilities. These worries reduce productivity and employers are experimenting with services that assist employees in finding the services their aging parents require and sometimes even provide day care for the elderly. Working women should find that the enlightened employer may provide them with extra benefits that assist them in balancing their many life responsibilities with work responsibilities. It may pay to shop around and compare benefits.

Small Businesses Creating Jobs

Another major trend is the growth of small business. It used to be that the large corporation provided the largest proportion of new jobs. Now those corporations are downsizing and laying off their employees. Companies with 100 or fewer employees will generate up to half the new jobs in the 90's. The Fortune 500 companies in the 1980's cut about 3.5 million jobs while small business added about 20 million.[1] This means that you should seriously look at the smaller company. You may find that the atmosphere in a smaller company may provide you with a more ideal work environment: less company politics, the ability to understand the entire company and how to be effective in it. More opportunities for advancement may exist in smaller companies. Women may find it is easier to get promoted because of the lack of an old-boys network in the company hierarchy and few management structures to work under.

Demand for Services

With almost 60 percent of married and single women working, the demand for services to support these women is growing. They need their houses cleaned, children cared for, meals cooked, groceries bought, parents cared for, and other services. The innovative women can capitalize on this trend by coming up with a unique service that working women will want to purchase to make their life easier.

Of Course, Computers

Don't forget about computers. Being computer literate is almost a given in careers today. A woman who has been out of the work place for some time needs to learn computer skills to re-enter. Even with other credentials that have stood the test of time, the addition of computer skills will be an asset.

Some Geographic Areas Do Better

We are continuing to see the trend where geographic location plays a role in employability. Some parts of the U.S. have been harder hit by the recent recession than others. States like Nebraska have a 4.1% job growth rate with construction, dairy products and education being part of their expanding industries. Arkansas has a job growth rate of 3.3% with the growth in textiles, machinery, and business services. Idaho has a job growth rate of 2.5% with growth in business services, recreation, and government. Utah has a growth rate of 2.4% with job growth in construction, transportation, and legal services.[2] If you can find regions and occupations that are growing higher than the country average, you might consider relocating to an area with a healthier economy.

Use of Temporary Employees

Another trend which is changing the nature of work is the use of temporaries, consultants, and part-timers. This helps companies keep their headcounts down, reduces their benefits costs and retains flexibility to add temporary help when needed. For the employee, this means attractive benefits packages are not available but it also gives the employee flexibility and freedom to do one job for awhile and then move on to another. For some, this freedom and flexibility may make up for the downside of lack of benefits. Some temporary employees may not need the benefits, receiving them from their spouse, or there may be options available where a temporary worker can buy into a group plan. Some of the higher paid professional temporaries may find that medical benefits are provided.

The pay scale has changed dramatically for temporary workers. Ten years ago temporaries were paid minimum wage. Today the average wage for a clerical temp is about $8 an hour. A professional temp can make as much as $40 to $50 an hour.[3]

The temporary work industry grew at an average of 10 percent of annual payroll between 1987 and 1989. Temporary workers are primarily employed as clericals. The rest of temporaries are almost evenly divided between industrial, technical, management and professional, and medical support.

Many employees laid off from larger corporations are finding that the only way they can re-enter the business world is as an independent consultant providing a niche service to companies that formerly would have hired them fulltime or had employed them. Though job security is gone, under closer scrutiny you will find that there is no such thing as a safe, secure job in today's world. All jobs could be gone tomorrow and the individual who assumes an attitude of being a self-entrepreneur, employed or self-employed, will be able to deal with this change better.

Areas for Growth

Based on these trends, we can develop a list of opportunities for jobs with the largest job growth, the fastest growing jobs, and the emerging jobs of the future. No one has a crystal ball, of course, and can predict with accuracy. The key for the worker is to have a higher level of education or training than was formerly required to get a good job. At the same time, the education or training should not be too specialized so that you can make job changes without having to become a fulltime student. In 1987, 45.4% of employed workers had better than a high school degree. By the year 2000, this percentage will be up to 54.4%.[4]

Some of the fastest growing jobs will be: medical assistants, home health aides, radiological technologists and technicians, medical secretaries, securities and financial services sales workers, travel agents, computer systems analysts, computer programmers, human services workers, corrections officers and jailers, electrical and electronics engineers, and receptionist and information clerks.

The largest job growth will occur in retail and service fields like health care, computers and legal work. We are seeing a reduction of new jobs in the blue collar jobs as foreign companies with lower labor costs pick up those jobs.

We can look at technological advances and predict that what we might consider an obscure or non-existent profession today may boom in the future. Areas where we will see emerging careers will be the fields of: computers and electronics, robotics and artificial intelligence, the energy industry, the information industry, the ocean industry, and space transportation. Some of these jobs include aquaculturist, artificial intelligence cyborg mechanic, free lance librarian, information broker, lunar technician, marine transportation economist, ocean farmer, plate tectonics technician, robot programmer and tectonic statistician.[5] Some of these jobs sound like they are from a science fiction story, but then look at today's world. Who would have predicted how the personal computer would revolutionize the world thirty years ago? Who would have predicted even ten years ago that more than $1 billion dollars would be spent in 1992 on assisted reproductive services for couples unable to conceive naturally?

Jobs with the largest job growth are less exotic however. According to the U.S. Bureau of Labor, these jobs include: retail salespersons, registered nurses, janitors and cleaners, waiters and waitresses, general managers and top executives, general office clerks, secretaries (except legal and medical, which are in the fastest growing category), nursing aides, orderlies and attendants, truck drivers, receptionists and information clerks, cashiers, guards, computer programmers, food counter, fountain and related workers, food preparation workers, licensed practical nurses, school teachers, computer systems analysts, accountants and auditors, general utility maintenance repairers, child care workers, gardeners and groundskeepers, lawyers, electrical and electronics engineers, carpenters, sales floor stock clerks, food service and lodging managers, home health aides, restaurant cooks, physicians, teachers aides, clerical supervisors and managers, blue collar worker supervisor, electrical and electronic engineering technicians, dining room and cafeteria attendants and bar helpers, financial managers, automotive mechanics, medical secretaries and social workers.[6]

These jobs reflect the shift from manufacturing to a service and information society and with more people working, we need more services in all areas to manage our lives.

Watch Out for Opportunities

The message is clear. What are considered good jobs today will change in the future. You have to consider how the world around you is changing. Statistics tell us that the average person changes careers three times in their lifetime. The need to change careers comes from the world around you. Keep your eyes and ears open so that these changes around you create opportunities for you as it becomes clear that your services will no longer be needed in one area but that opportunity exists in another.

RECOMMENDATIONS FOR FURTHER WORK

1. Make it a habit to read weekly and monthly magazines, paying particular attention to information about trends. Go to the library and review a wide selection of magazines to begin to get a feel for how the world is changing.
2. If you are considering post-high school education, call the schools and ask them what the hottest fields for their graduates are and the placement records for their programs. All schools maintain records on placement of their graduates.

[1]Harkavy, Michael. *101 Careers: A Guide to the Fastest-Growing Opportunities.* New York: John Wiley & Sons, Inc., 1990.
[2] *"Where the Jobs Are", Newsweek,* January 20, 1992, pp. 42-44.
[3] "Firms find flexibility in temporary employees," *Eau Claire Leader-Telegram,* February 23, 1992, p. 4D.
[4] Harkavy, Michael.
[5] Feingold, S Norman. *Emerging Careers: New Occupations for the Year 2000 and Beyond.* Garret Park, MD: Garrett Park Press, 1983.
[6] U.S. Bureau of the Census, *Statistical Abstract of the United State: 1990 (110th edition.)* Washington, DC, 1990, p. 398.

Chapter Seven

How Employers Handle Arrest and Conviction Records and Credit History

If you are starting fresh, after a turbulent personal history and record, there are some things you should know about provisions in the law in regard to arrest and conviction records. This information should put your mind at ease regarding your ability to make a fresh start and become responsible and employed.

There are many federal laws pertaining to how employers may treat employees from the time they are hired to the time they leave employment. This chapter does not attempt to give a detailed analysis nor go into additional laws at the state level which provide additional protection to employees and applicants. It does attempt to cover in a succinct and general manner the general treatment you can expect around arrest and conviction records and credit history.

Job Related Only

Issues which govern how a potential employer treats arrest and conviction records include job-relatedness, business necessity and whether arrest and conviction records are related to a bona-fide occupational qualification. In other words, unless the arrest or conviction record would deal with a work-related job duty, it is not relevant. The reason this is so is because an employer's use of arrest and conviction records may have a discriminatory impact on minority groups. Therefore, federal and state laws largely limit a potential employer inquiring about arrests and convictions or using any information about arrests or convictions in making employment decisions.

An employer can ask about your arrest or convictions if it is related to the job duties. An applicant convicted of embezzlement applying for a bank teller's position could be excluded from the job because of the applicability of the conviction to job-related duties pertaining to money.

Treatment Different for Convictions

Arrest records and conviction records can be treated slightly differently because an arrest does not necessarily mean charges were filed. Even if charged, a person may have been acquitted. If asking for conviction information, the employer has a responsibility to consider the seriousness of the crime (whether a felony or misdemeanor), the frequency of the convictions, the time lapsed between the application and the conviction, and the age of the applicant when he or she was convicted.

If the employer is collecting the information because it is job-related, some state laws also limit the availability of applicant's history within the company. Access to that information may be restricted to one focal point within the company. That individual is responsible for weighing the information and deciding how it relates to the job duties. These restrictions on how widely information may be disseminated help maintain the applicant's privacy.

Garnishment and Credit History

It is worth noting that information obtained on garnishment and credit history may also be discriminatory. Therefore an employer can not inquire about credit history or financial history without substantiating that it is job-related.

Fresh Start Possible

Any woman who wishes to make a fresh start can begin the job search with peace of mind that her past, under state and federal laws, is protected by fairness and privacy concerns. Of course there is no guarantee that you will not be discriminated against because of a an arrest or conviction record. However, your job search should be made easier by knowing what your rights are. If it becomes clear to you that you will be discriminated against in your community, you should consider relocating to a city or town where you are not known and could make a fresh start, or you should consider taking legal steps to redress the treatment you have received. This country allows individuals to change and overcome their past.

RECOMMENDATIONS FOR FURTHER WORK

1. If you have had problems in the past, consider how you will respond to questions about your past. A sincere truthful response is always the best policy. Preparing for these questions will help you respond most effectively.
2. Locate individuals who are responsible and would be willing to serve as references. It is better to have your list developed before you go job hunting. Many employers no longer check personal references, but should it be necessary to provide a reference, you will be prepared. Consider past employers, co-workers, teachers, ministers/pastors/clergy, civic leaders and volunteer associates as potential references.

Chapter Eight

Resumes: Summing Up What You Offer A Potential Employer

This chapter on resumes has been included for several reasons. You may need to get a job right now. A resume is a marketing tool which presents your knowledge, skills, and abilities to a potential employer. A resume can also help you summarize what you're offering, improving your opinion of yourself. A resume also forces you to seriously think about your career goals for the future.

Regardless of whether or not you are actively looking for a job right now, every person should have a current resume. When an opportunity does arise, if your resume is prepared, all you have to do is pull it out, update it, retype it, and you're ready to write a cover letter or take it with you for the interview. Another important reason for keeping your resume updated is that you keep it current, capturing all of your recent accomplishments, activities, and job duties in an accurate manner. If you don't keep it current, you will be likely to forget something that might be critical to getting you the next and better position you want.

Entire books have been devoted to the subject of resumes. While the resume is important, it is something that must be seen in perspective. A resume is used by a potential employer to screen candidates for the job opening. A resume presents your qualifications so that employers will select you for an interview if you match the position requirements. The purpose of a resume is to get you a job interview. Without the interview, you cannot sell yourself. If the employer does not have a job opening and you send a resume, it is unlikely they will interview or hire you.

Resume Rules

There are some rules about resumes that are very important:

1. The resume should be no longer than one to two pages.
2. The resume should be neat.
3. There should be no misspellings or typographical errors on the resume, regardless of the type of position you are applying for.
4. Every resume you submit should be an original. It is likely that once your resume has passed the initial screening, a copy of it will be made and sent to several hiring supervisors or managers. If you sent an original to the company, the copy made will be legible and clean looking. If you sent a copy, the company will copy your copy, and quality begins to deteriorate at that point.

Three Types of Resumes

There are three types of resumes: chronological, functional, and a combination of the two previous approaches. A chronological resume combines the experience and employment history under one section. Each position is listed by job title, dates of employment, company name, city, and state, followed by a description of job duties. This format is a good one to use if you have a steady employment record, and/or are seeking a job in a career that is already established. Employers and interviewers like this format because it is easy to follow and helps them decide quickly whether an interview would be appropriate. Most resumes are scanned quickly and a decision is made within 30 to 60 seconds whether or not your skills are a good match for the job opening.

A functional resume highlights skills without detailing specific positions held. A functional resume allows you to stress selected areas of employment. It can also help lessen the impact of a spotty employment record. It can be used effectively if you are changing careers or if you lack direct job-related experience. If you have considerable work experience, a functional resume can serve to emphasize the skills and achievements which relate most directly to the jobs you are applying for.

However, functional resumes are regarded with skepticism because the person may be covering up a job gap that is difficult or uncomfortable to explain. One way to get around that objection is to use a combination approach, listing your job history in a section following your skills section which succinctly lists your employment history without a detailed description of the experience.

How Resumes Are Handled

Your resume may be screened by someone besides the hiring manager: a secretary, a personnel clerk, an administrator or a hiring committee. Make it as clear as possible how your qualifications match the position requirements so that your chances of getting into the pile of resumes that are sent on to the hiring manager or supervisor are better. You can do this by how you describe your job experience as well as the position objective which you have listed at the top of the resume.

Use a Cover Letter

Always use a cover letter to accompany your resume. This allows you to explain what position you are applying for, how you heard about it, why you are enthusiastic about the job, and an opportunity to write a brief summary of what you have to offer the employer. Use the listing of skills required from the advertisement for the job or the job listing and briefly show how you meet them. A cover letter should not be long. The letter should be individualized for each position you are applying for. A cover letter also helps direct your resume to the right person in the organization who is hiring individuals with your skills.

What a Resume Contains

A resume contains sections that deal with:

—your name, address, phone number

—your position objective

—your job experience, paid or unpaid

—your education

—your achievements: special skills, knowledge of equipment or procedures, honors received, memberships, etc.

—special interests that demonstrate originality, drive, ability to be part of a team

Now let's go over each section individually.

Name, Address, and Phone Number

Legislation now makes it illegal for the employer to ask how old you are, your race, your age and your marital status. Therefore, all you need is the above information. It is not a good idea to volunteer other information because employers are not supposed to keep those records.

If you don't have a permanent phone number, find a friend, family member, or organization that will take a message for you and tell them how to respond to the call. For instance, they could reply, "So and so isn't available, but will be calling in to pick up messages. May I have her return your call?" Then you take responsibility for making sure that you do call in every day to see if there are any messages. Often an interview is set up in a short time frame with several potential candidates, and if you are not available, you've lost an opportunity to interview and perhaps get the job. Most employers are interested in talking to all of their identified potential job candidates to the extent that they will set up an interview time that meets your needs, after work if you are working now, or at a time when child care is available, or school not in session for you.

Your Position Objective

This section may have to be changed with each resume you send out, depending on your level of skill. This section tells the employer that you are interested in a specific type of job. It can be general enough to not eliminate a potential match but it tells the employer that you are focused. It will tell the employer where you want to go.

Your objective should be work-centered, and your goal stated in terms of position title, job function, or skills required to do the job. For example, a position title objective would say: "Electronics Technician." A functional skills objective would say: "Position of supervision in retail sales with responsibility for scheduling, ordering, displays." Or an objective written in terms of skills would say: "Position that requires knowledge of WordPerfect, Dbase, and Lotus." Make sure your position objective matches the job opening you are applying for. If it does not, the employer may feel that you are applying for many different jobs out of desperation not because you want that particular job.

Your Job Experience

Start with your current or most recent employer and work back in time. State the job title, dates of employment and a description of job duties. Then give the employer's name, address, and phone number. If the job was ten years ago in New Hampshire, and you now live in California, simply stating the company's name and city and state is probably sufficient. You want to highlight the most important duties, not every duty accomplished. Here you will find it useful to use active, strong words similar to what are used on job descriptions. A list of "did" words is included at the end of this chapter. Also included are words that stress certain aspects of your character. Flip to the back of this chapter and take time to look at these words.

Remember Your Unpaid Experiences As Well

Some of you may find that your volunteer and unpaid experience is significant, even more so than your paid experience. Use the same approach you would take if the work was paid. Find a suitable job title, and list the duties that accompanied the volunteer experience. Consider any participation in school, church, and community activities as possibilities for inclusion. Your involvement heading the church's annual financial drive, serving as newsletter editor for your club, volunteering as a scouting leader or participating in Toastmasters speaks volumes about your skills and abilities. Use as many of your life experiences as you can to provide a complete and thorough picture of your value to a future employer.

A listing of words follows which may help you succinctly capture your experiences in words that employers recognize as being useful to them. Review the list and use these words to capture your experiences as a volunteer and from life experiences.

Sample Listing of Skills Acquired Either Through Paid or Non-Work Experience

Supervisory Skills
Leading
Instructing
Organizing people, data, things
Negotiating
Delegating responsibility
Motivating others
Evaluating people and data
Implementing
Coordinating
Planning
Assigning
Scheduling

Money Management Skills
Analyzing
Comparison shopping
Recordkeeping
Purchasing
Budgeting
Mathematical
Estimating
Forecasting

Creative Skills
Interior decorating
Painting, drawing
Sewing
Designing
Crocheting, knitting, needlework
Detailing

Color coordination
Innovative
Inventive
Remodeling
Gardening
Spatial relations

Communications Skills
Speaking before a group
Listening
Writing
Spelling
Effective one-to-one conversation
Rapport with others
Counseling

Interpersonal Skills
Friendly
Assertive
Adaptive
Confident
Relate well to others

Teaching Skills
Developing curriculum
Designing curriculum
Instructing

Parenting Skills
Nurturing
Counseling
Understanding
Nursing
Disciplining
Advising

Motivating

Educational History

Again start with the most recent education and work back in time. List diplomas, certificates, associate degrees or college degrees from most recent back to high school, Include short courses that are relevant.

Your Achievements

Here you can list what equipment you have operated in the past, any certifications you have earned, honors you have received, memberships that are relevant in the job search. If you have kept a folder in which to put in notes, clippings, or correspondence about these activities, you will be more likely to remember them.

If you haven't, go through your scrapbooks and files to refresh your memory. Now is a good time to begin keeping a file marked "personal" to keep all your accomplishments organized in one place. Place newspaper clippings, letters of thanks, correspondence, copies of club minutes, grade reports, whatever documentation will help you remember what you have accomplished in your life.

Special Interests

The distinction between your achievements and special interests is that special interests represent accomplishments from your personal life. Let us say that you have always been interested in antiques and have specialized in collecting postcards of your community between 1900 and 1950. That hobby would be something to include because it shows your unique interests and ability to organize a project. Perhaps you've enjoyed crafts. Put that down if you think it might be relevant.

It may be that the job requires fine hand movement and good eye sight and your special interests would tell them that you are skilled in that area. Or let's say you have actively participated in community affairs and have always volunteered to help set up the community's Christmas display or participated in the annual spring cleanup. This says that you work hard to achieve a goal that is meaningful to you and are community-minded. Put it down and it may select you into an interview.

Take Your Time

If the task of putting together a resume for the first time appears to be overwhelming, then nibble at it. Rough it out one session, then look up dates, phone numbers, addresses another time. Add the job duties and refine your words until you feel it represents you in the most professional, highest quality manner. Use the work sheets at the end of the chapter to capture everything you want to include in your resume.

After you have typed it or had it typed, read and reread it to be sure there are no misspellings or typographical errors. Then give it to a family member or friend for proofreading. Any employer will throw out a resume of someone who meets the job qualifications simply because of misspellings or typographical mistakes. These things tell the employer that you are sloppy, are not interested in checking your work, or that you don't know how to write clearly and accurately. Job skill requirements are changing and almost everyone needs to know how to communicate on paper.

Alternatives to Preparing It Yourself

Almost every city has a desktop publisher or printer that can help you prepare an attractive resume. Using their computer and printer, you can have a professional looking resume for a reasonable fee. Look under "Resume Service" in the phone book to find those companies offering this service.

You can also rent a computer at some printing shops for a small hourly rental fee and have access to equipment that you might not have at home.

Software Alternatives

If you do have a computer, you might benefit from purchasing a software package that prepares resumes. "Resumemaker" by Individual Software, for example, lists for $49.95. It contains numerous resume formats, guide letters, a word processor with spell checker, action word glossary, target company database, activities log, appointment calendar, and tips for interviewing and job hunting activities. "ResumExpert" by A Lasting Impression also prepares resumes by supplying different templates. This one also lists for about $50 and you can purchase a separate package to prepare cover letters. There are many other packages available.

Resume Appearance

Select a high quality paper and a simple typeface for your final copy. In general, the paper should be white, ivory, or light gray for an especially conservative appearance. Typeface styles that are readable and simple include: New Century Schoolbook, Times, and Helvetica.

Good paper choices are parchment, classic linen, or classic laid. A visit to an office supply company will allow you to select the right paper and also purchase matching envelopes. Don't underestimate the importance of resume and cover letter appearance in making a good impression.

It's Not Really Difficult

If you have never prepared a resume before, relying only on job applications to obtain prior employment, this chapter may have seemed complicated. Preparing a resume is like any life skill. Once you have done it, the task doesn't seem so difficult. Preparing a resume should become second nature after you have taken the time to put together your first one. You will understand that a resume is a marketing tool to show what you have to offer a potential employer. Study the sample at the end of the chapter. Then turn to the resume worksheet and start preparing your own resume. Remember to concentrate on where you are going, not where you have been, and the task will be easier as you work towards achieving your exciting plans for your future. You will learn how to present yourself in the most effective manner in a very short period of time, and your hard work will reap future dividends.

RECOMMENDATIONS FOR FURTHER WORK

1. Keep your resume updated. Even if you're not now looking for a new job, type up a new resume so that you'll be ready if something should come up. In the process of reviewing your past job history, education, and other accomplishments, you may learn something about your career direction.
2. Begin your "personal accomplishments" file. Put in the clippings from your community and religious involvement. Save letters from your boss and others complimenting you on a job well done. If you take a class, put the grade report in your file. All these reminders will help you remember what to include to present yourself thoroughly.

Descriptive Words

These are good words to describe the qualities you possess. These words can be used in cover letters and in interviews to market your qualities.

If you want to stress your ability to handle details, try these words: **detail-minded, precise, accurate, orderly, efficient, meets all due dates.**

If you want to create a positive impact, use these words: **actively, administered, completed, developed, effected, implemented, increased, reduced, simplified, solved.**

If you want to stress your ability to assume responsibility, use these words: **created, devised, generated, initiated, streamlined, revamped, shaped and directed, strong dedication to, originated, closely supervised.**

If you want to indicate your desire to get ahead, use these words: **perform well under pressure, self-motivated, accept responsibility, enthusiastic, a commitment to, action-oriented.**

If you want to show a capacity for reasoning and understanding, use these words: **ability to think analytically, probing mind, fast-thinking, perceptive, creative, ideas person.**

If you want to show that you are profit-minded, use these words: **results-oriented, reduced excessive costs, controlled spiralling costs, adept at saving money, simplified procedures, generated cost savings.**

Other words to use:
ability
adaptable
adept
aggressive
alert
ambitious

analytical
attentive
broad-minded
competent
conscientious
consistent
constructive
creative
dependable
detail-minded
determined
diplomatic
disciplined
diversified
economical
effective
efficient
energetic
enterprising
enthusiastic
fair
forceful
imaginative
independent
instrumental
knowledgeable
logical
loyal
mature
methodical
objective
optimistic
perceptive
personable
personally

pertinent
pleasant
positive
practical
productive
proficient
qualified
realistic
reliable
resourceful
responsible
self-reliant
sincere
substantially
successfully
systematic
tactful
talented
technical
versatile
vigorous

Resume Worksheet

Employment Objective ______________

____

____

____

____

Experience History

1. Job Title ______________________
Job Duties ______________________

____

____

____

____

____

Where ______________________

____

When ______________________

2. Job Title ______________________________
Job Duties ______________________________
____
____
____
____
____
____
Where ______________________________
When ______________________________
3. Job Title:
Job Duties: ______________________________
____
____
____
____
____
Where: ______________________________
When: ______________________________

4 Job Title: ______________________________
Job Duties: ______________________________
____
____
____
____
____
Where:
When: ______________________________
____

5. Other Work Experience: List job titles/positions you want to show but do not want to go into detail about, i.e., short term jobs, part-time jobs, etc.

6. Military Experience: (optional and if not used elsewhere on this resume)

Job Title:

Job Duties:

Branch of Military

Where:

When:

7. Special Achievements: Awards, Licenses, Certifications, etc.

8. Special Skills:

_ _

_ _

_ _

_ _

_ _

9. Hobbies

_ _

_ _

_ _

_ _

_ _

_ _

10. Education:

Technical School and/or College: _ _ _ _ _ _ _ _ _ _ _
Where: _ _ _ _ _ _ _ When _ _ _ _ _ _ _ _ _ _ _
Degree/Certificate or courses taken: _ _ _ _ _ _ _ _ _ _

High School: _ _ _ _ _ _ _ _ _ _ _ _ _ _ _ _ _ _ _
Where: _ _ _ _ _ _ _ _ _ When _ _ _ _ _ _ _ _ _ _
Diploma or courses taken: _ _ _ _ _ _ _ _ _ _ _ _ _

"Did" Words

These are strong verbs to describe previous job experience or experience gained from volunteer activities. Use on resumes, applications, and in cover letters.

accelerated
accomplished
achieved
adapted
administered
analyzed
approved
assisted
built
checked
compared
compiled
completed
conceived
conducted
constructed
controlled
conveyed
coordinated
created
delegated
demonstrated
designed
developed
devised
directed
effected
eliminated
established
evaluated

exceeded
expanded
expedited
fabricated
facilitated
filed
formulated
found
gathered
generated
guided
implemented
improved
increased
influenced
initiated
inspected
installed
instructed
insured
interpreted
introduced
launched
lectured
led
loaded
maintained
managed
manipulated
mastered
measured
motivated
moved
negotiated
observed
operated

organized
originated
participated
performed
persuaded
pinpointed
planned
prepared
produced
programmed
promoted to
proved
provided
ran
read
reconciled
recorded
recruited
reduced
reinforced
removed
reorganized
repaired
researched
restructured
revamped
reviewed
revised
scheduled
simplified
separated
set up
solved
spearheaded
structured
streamlined

stocked
studied
supervised
supported
taped
taught
tended
trained
translated
transported
turned-around
typed
updated
used
won
wrote

Sample Resume

Sally Smith
100 A Street
Anytown, MN
505/555-1212

Position Objective: To use desktop publishing design and writing skills in an editorial position.

EXPERIENCE

Editor, P.T.O. Newsletter, First Elementary School, Anytown, MN, September, 1989-Present.
Designed and edited on a volunteer basis this quarterly publication sent to 800 parents of the elementary school. Developed the newsletter format, created and managed a reporter system, and edited, wrote and laid out the six page publication in a timely manner using Quark Xpress on a Macintosh II system.

Office Assistant, Outdoor Activities, Inc., Anytown, MN, January, 1985-September, 1989.
Provided secretarial support to store management and sales staff of this recreational equipment merchandiser. Assisted in the development of a quarterly newsletter on outdoor recreational activities, developed a database of customers for newsletter mailing and wrote some of the stories. Used PageMaker software on a Macintosh system to design the newsletter. Also responsible for invoicing, ordering, phones, and general typing.

Secretary, Town Crier, Anytown, MN, December, 1983 - December, 1985.
Provided secretarial support to general manager of this daily newspaper. Duties included typing, answering the phone, setting up appointments, and taking minutes at newspaper and association meetings. Occasionally reported on city council meetings.

EDUCATION

Administrative Assistant Degree, Anytown Technical School, Anytown, MN, September, 1981- May, 1983. Gradepoint average: 3.75 (4.0 total possible).

High School Diploma, Anytown High School, Anytown, MN, June, 1981.

Desktop publishing and design courses, including: "Introduction to PageMaker," "Advanced Desktop Publishing," and "Layout and Design, 101," Anytown Technical School, 1983-1985.

ACHIEVEMENTS

Named "TOP PARENT PARTNER," First Elementary P.T.O., May, 1990, for newsletter to parents.

Received "Most Promising Student" Scholarship, Kiwanis, 1981.

SPECIAL INTERESTS

Drawing and painting, using water colors and acrylics. Taken many art courses to make hobby more challenging.

Work displayed at Public Library, Winter, 1991.

Won blue ribbon for acrylic titled "Blue Ice" Regional Anytown Art Fair, September, 1989.

Chapter Nine

Job Search Strategies

If you're not currently employed, it may be comforting to know that the average length of time it takes to secure a job is a little less than four months. Of course, that's an average. Some individuals may find it takes two years and someone else one week. Despite all the bad economic headlines, there is a constant need for new workers. Even a company that is laying off workers may be hiring because they need employees with different skill sets.

Statistics also tell us, according to the National Bureau for Economic Research, that the average American worker holds 10 different jobs, lasting an average of 3.6 years. Workers will have two or three different careers in the course of their lifetime.

Because of these statistics, you will benefit from improving your job-hunting skills and understanding the potential sources for your next position. The statistics tell you that you will go job-hunting many times in your lifetime.

Job Hunting Skills

Job hunting skills include analyzing your work history and presenting yourself effectively in a resume, writing cover letters, participating effectively in a job interview, and knowing the proper sources to find a job. Your local federal and state job service office probably offers a short course in job hunting skills. You should enroll in the course. The few hours of time will be well spent and you will probably learn one or two things you did not know. You can also read books on all aspects of job hunting. Many books go into great detail on each aspect of the job hunt. Read a few so that you can sharpen your skills.

Take advantage of all the free resources located in your community that might help you analyze your work history and present yourself in the best light. More than likely, your local higher education institutions offer individual counseling and group sessions so that your job hunting skills can be improved. Take advantage of them! You'll learn something new with every activity you undertake and it just might be the piece of advice that will help you get your next and better position.

Major Job Sources

The major sources for finding jobs are: using the classified ads, private employment agencies, federal/state employment services, school/college placement services, civil service, and networking with friends, relatives and teachers. Yet a job-seeker should not limit herself to these sources. We know, for instance, that only 24% of job openings appear in the classified section, and sometimes those ads are not bonafide openings. They are put in to broaden the pool of applicants for Affirmative Action/EEO requirements. Private employment agencies charge a fee, which might or might not be paid by the employer. Paying a fee, however, might be cost effective if it reduces the amount of time you spend looking for work. Federal and state employment services are usually swamped by clients, with the number of job-seekers larger than the number of jobs. We know that one job offer is made for every 1,470 resumes mailed out—a discouraging ratio. But those sources work for some. Not everyone realizes there are other ways to secure employment. If you're serious about finding a job, you will work at it as if it is a job and will consider other avenues to help you locate the best job for you. If you use a combination of many different sources, you are more likely to find a job sooner. Using different sources increases the likelihood that you will be at the right place at the right time; luck is a factor in finding a position.

Additional Job Sources

For instance, consider a cold canvass, both in person and on the telephone. A cold canvass consists of contacting your local businesses and industries to find out if they have a vacancy appropriate to your skills and interest. All you have to lose is your time. When you conduct a cold canvass, state the kind of skills you possess so that they can respond to your question if they have a need now or in the near future for someone with your skills. Have your resume prepared and ready to hand out if you canvass in person. Allow enough time to fill out a job application on the spot. When filling out the job application, take a few minutes to scan it first, before you start filling it out. Respond to all the questions, and if they don't apply, write, "Does not apply" rather than simply leaving it blank. Most organizations will require that you fill out an application in addition to your resume. Don't be discouraged if nothing turns up. One of those leads might pay off at some point in the future.

If efforts to secure a fulltime position fail, consider part-time work. A part-time job has the potential of becoming fulltime. Also consider temporary or summer work. These provide experience and an introduction to an employer's organization. You may find that the temporary work can lead to permanent work, and you have gained valuable work experience.

Join a job search club. Many groups exist today, especially in cities where unemployment has been chronic. These groups will help keep your spirits up and morale high and you will learn a lot about the local employment picture.

Inquire at your local social agencies to see if they provide any placement services that you might quality for.

County and city governments generally maintain personnel offices. File your application with both. Contact federal and state civil service offices and find out how you can find out about openings and apply for those that interest you. The benefits packages with public employment are generally excellent, especially retirement and health benefits.

If you are currently employed, don't forget about the internal job posting system at your company to help you find a better job. Talk to your personnel office, and make it a habit to check the openings posted on the bulletin board.

If there are professional magazines in your field, review the job openings in the publication on a regular basis. Find out if the professional or trade association has a job finder service and sign up for it.

Look in your phone book in the yellow pages under "Employment Agencies" and "Employment Contractors" and "Employment Training Services." Be acquainted with all those organizations and understand what they offer and make sure you are registered with them. A simple phone call could lead to much more.

The Job Interview

The purpose of the job search is to turn up openings and obtain job interviews with those organizations that are hiring. The more job interviews you have, the more likely you will get a job offer. Once a potential employer has a chance to see you in the flesh, the more likely you are to be hired.

Preparation for the job interview will help you be calm about the interview. Most employers expect some nervousness during the job interview so don't worry about being nervous. By practicing your responses to interview questions, you can reduce your nervousness considerably. Most employers today use a patterned interview approach. The patterned interview is based on the premise that the most likely predictor of future success on the job is past successes you have had. The interviewer is going to ask you a lot of open-ended questions (questions that require a response of several sentences or paragraphs rather than a simple yes or no response) to help gather the information they need to make their decision about the most likely candidate for the job.

Here is where you will have a chance to sell yourself. Women have a tendency to sell themselves short. You have much to offer and it is up to you to communicate your assets. Practice your response to these questions:

—Tell me about yourself?

—How did you happen to become interested in our company?

—What are your current job expectations? What are your job expectations for the future?

—Describe your last job. What were your duties and responsibilities?

—Which job function did you like best? Why?

—What were some of your major accomplishments? Why were they challenging?

—How have your previous jobs prepared you for this position?

—What courses interested you most in school?

—What elective did you take?

—What, if any, are your future educational plans?

—How has your training and education prepared you for this job?

—What do you see as your major strengths?

—What do you see as your major weaknesses?

—What do you feel you can bring to this job?

—Which of your skills or abilities do you feel could stand improvement?

—Tell me about a time when you were most frustrated by your work and how you handled it?

—In general, how do you evaluate your ability to keep several things going simultaneously?

—Why did you leave your last job?

—How would you describe yourself?

—Why should we hire you?

—Do you have any questions?

Always try in your responses to clarify what your skills and abilities are. Make sure the interviewer knows what you have to offer. Stress that you are a hard worker and willing to learn and that you really want the job. Be sincere.

Laws govern what employers may not ask as well. In general if it's job related, it's legal. If it is not job related, it's illegal. You may find employers asking illegal questions anyway and you should think about how you wish to respond to those questions. One potential response is, "I thought about how I would answer that if you should ask it. I choose to tell you...." This communicates in a positive way that you are in control of your response and also makes you feel good.

Even though you have had a job interview, get going right after the interview to line up another interview. By maintaining your job search momentum, you won't be discouraged when a job interview does not result in a position. Too many job seekers interview, cease looking while they wait for a decision, and when they do not get the job, go through a grief process before they finally get going again. It is much easier psychologically to deal with a rejection if you have several potential offers to choose from. Keep looking until you are absolutely certain you have a job. The more interviews you have, the greater your chances of finding a job.

RECOMMENDATIONS FOR FURTHER WORK

1. Practice your response to the interview questions. Have a family member or friends play the role of interviewer.
2. Pretend you are an advertising copy writer trying to sell yourself. Think up and list all your good qualities and accomplishments. Refer to this list before you go on an interview.
3. Every day when you are searching for a job, use a different job search strategy. That way you will be sure to have covered all the bases.
4. Plan your wardrobe for the job interview before the interview day. You can wear the same outfit each time you have an interview. You should wear something dressy. Dress appropriately for the position you are interviewing for. NEVER WEAR JEANS! If the job is a trade or skill job,

you probably could wear a more casual outfit, such as dress pants and top. For office-type jobs, wear a skirt and blouse, dress, or suit to the interview. Polish your shoes. Look neat and clean, especially your hands. Keep make-up looking natural. Save wild hair styles and jewelry for your personal life.

Chapter Ten

Putting It All Together

Why some individuals are successful at implementing a career plan that makes them happy and others seem to spend their working years unhappy and dissatisfied partially comes from the inherent difficulties in career planning. As a human being, you tend to resist change. You know the world is changing and that you need to adapt to it, but your current life and existing relationships sometimes make it hard to see future possibilities. Limited by your lack of information about career opportunities, you may do nothing and lose out. Even when you take a risk, the difficulty of knowing whether this is the right thing to do creates anxiety and fear in you. You also find it difficult to translate your individual needs into organization goals and when that difficulty is combined with the fact that you are not always the best judge of your personal strengths and weaknesses, you may become bogged down in indecision.

Make Career Planning Career/Life Planning

Perhaps if you viewed career planning as part of life planning you would be more successful. Ideally life/career planning is a process, not an event. It should be something you always have on your mind, even when you are happily working because changes occur in you and the world and the job you loved so much today can become one you despise tomorrow. If you keep a higher self-awareness level, those changes are less likely to creep up on you and startle you with the realization and question of "How did I ever let this happen to me?"

If you viewed life/career planning as a process of implementing your own self-concept and values you would lessen the probability of finding yourself trapped and angry that you are doing something so devoid of meaning. You would make decisions more consciously and listen to your inner voice as to what the best decision is for you.

If you considered yourself responsible for your future and not a victim, you would feel in charge of your life and make sure that you had information to help you make decisions.

You would regard the key question as being what to do to be successful at life, not simply successful at work, and follow your own guides as to what success constitutes. The result is having your personal, spiritual, and work lives in balance and in harmony with your values.

Trust Yourself

If you can learn to trust yourself you will have much greater success finding personal happiness. If you learn to trust yourself, you can learn to face risks despite feeling scared and anxious. You will be able to move along in your life and find the happiness and satisfaction you seek and deserve. The only way you can learn to trust yourself and take risks is to do just that and move through the feelings of fear, anxiety, and uncertainty that taking risks creates. Once you have worked through fear, anxiety and uncertainty one time, the next time you find yourself feeling more confident that you will get to the other side of your decision in good shape. It becomes easier and easier to be self-directed if you allow yourself the first step and trust in your ability to know what is best for you. Until you allow yourself to be self-directed you may find it hard to understand what it feels like or that it is a transition process that will unfold naturally if you allow it. You have to do it to see it, but sometimes it is the first step that gets in the way and prevents you from taking risks.

All of life is lived one step at a time, and very few mistakes or decisions are irretrievable or irrevocable. You can make course corrections; you can even make major paradigm shifts that dramatically change the way your life goes. You will find that you survive the change. It is the first step that is so hard. I hope this book helps you take the first step and guides you on a journey of finding fulfillment and satisfaction and happiness in work and life.

Bibliography

Banning, Kent. *Planning Your Career Changes. The Reasons, The Decisions, The Strategy*. Lincolnwood, IL: National Textbook Co., 1987.

Bond, Robert E. and Christopher E. Bond. *The Source Book of Franchise Opportunities*. Irwin, Inc.: Homewood, IL, 1992.

Carnevale, Anthony P. and Leila J. Gainer and Ann S. Meltzer. *Workplace Basics: The Skills Employers Want*. The American Society for Training and Development and The U.S. Department of Labor, Employment and Training Administration.

Csikszentmihalyi, Mihaly. *Flow: The Psychology of Optimal Experience*. New York: HarperPerennial, 1991.

Feingold, S. Norman. *Emerging Careers: New Occupations for the Year 2000 and Beyond*. Garret Park, MD: Garret Park Press, 1983.

Fritz, Robert M. *The Path of Least Resistance: Principles for Creating What You Want to Create*. Walpole, New Hampshire: Stillpoint Press, 1986.

Greenwood, Mary. *Hiring, Supervising and Firing Employees: An Employer's Guide to Discrimination Laws*. Wilmette, IL: Callaghan & Company, 1987.

Harkavy, Michael. *101 Careers: A Guide to the Fastest-Growing Opportunities*. New York: John Wiley & Sons, Inc., 1990.

Marino, Kim. *Just Resumes*. New York: John Wiley & Sons, Inc., 1991.

Outten, Wayne N. with Noah A. Kinigstein. *Rights of Employees: The Basic ACLU Guide to an Employee's Rights.* New York: Bantam, 1983.

Pollan, Stephen M. and Mark Levine. *The Field Guide to Starting a Business.* New York: Fireside Books, Simon and Schuster, Inc., 1990.

Taeuber, Cynthia. *Statistical Handbook on Women in America.* Phoenix, Arizona: Oryx Press.

Terkel, Studs. *People Talk About What They Do All Day and How They Feel About What They Do* . New York: Pantheon, 1972.

U.S. Bureau of the Census. *Statistical Abstract of the United States. 1991 (111th Edition.)* Washington, D.C. 1991.

Weiser, Marjorie P.K. and Jean S. Arbeiter. *Womanlist.* New York: Atheneum, 1981.